Yellowstone
Has
Teeth

Marjane Ambler

RIVERBEND
PUBLISHING

3 4 5 6 7 8 9 10 VP 20 19 18 17 16 15 14

ISBN 978-1-60639-063-4

Cover photo of Lamar Valley, Yellowstone National Park,
by Christopher Cauble, www.caublephotography.com
Cover and text design by Sarah Cauble, www.sarahcauble.com

RIVERBEND PUBLISHING
P.O. Box 5833
Helena, MT 59604
1-866-787-2363
www.riverbendpublishing.com

FSC
www.fsc.org
MIX
Paper from
responsible sources
FSC® C005010

Dedicated to Jerry and Cindy Mernin,
who made Yellowstone their home

Contents

Preface & Acknowledgments

In today's over-civilized world, people often long to escape the demands of everyday life and dream of a home on the frontier. When my husband and I wintered in Yellowstone National Park's isolated interior, there were times when my only interruption was a swan's shadow on my computer screen as it flew by my window. Our nine years of living year-round on the modern frontier also provided spurts of adrenalin. Snowmobiling among large mammals many times our size was only one of the challenges we faced.

Our story is about community as much as individuals. When we lived in Yellowstone in the late 1980s and early 1990s, there were no cell phones or email, and only limited television. We witnessed how the arrival of television dramatically changed the community dynamics. Through our experiences and interviews with others who lived in the park from the 1930s to the 1970s, we came to cherish our community and to be reminded that life on the frontier was about symbiosis and mutual dependence more than independence.

This book would have never happened without the encouragement—and criticism—of many friends and family members when they read various versions of the book over the past twenty years. In particular, the late Philippina Halstead told me in her inimitable, direct way, "Quit your day job and write that book!" After I quit my day job in southwest Colorado and moved back to Atlantic City, Wyoming, the Atlantic City Writers Group formed. Phil and the other members (Bob Townsend, Barbara Townsend, and Jo Trumble) gave me incentive to churn out chapters, and they spent hours offering their critiques.

Ranger Jerry Mernin read many of the chapters and provided factual corrections, advice about tone, and grammatical suggestions. It was a bit embarrassing for a lifelong journalist to get grammar lessons from a ranger, but Jerry was not just any ranger. His own memoir will be published soon. Cindy Mernin provided some of the most memorable slogans used in these pages, including "Paradise isn't for sissies." Grace Nutting provided the words used in the title: "Yellowstone has teeth."

My father, Edward Ambler, and his wife, Susie, helped ease our isolation by visiting us winter and summer, braving long snowmobile rides over Sylvan Pass and harrowing boat rides on Yellowstone Lake when many people their age would have stayed home.

Thanks to Nancy Gregory. Although she has lived and traveled, often alone, all over the Middle East and Africa, she validated our perceptions of danger in our adventures. Jazmyn McDonald, also a solo international traveler, helped me find the story arc and its significance. She reminded me there is a fundamental deception of every adventure story: Ninety percent of the journey is tedious, but the authors tell the parts that people want to hear.

A workshop on "The Hero's Journey" given by Gwynne Spencer in Cortez, Colorado, provided a framework to hang the material on, once I overcame my resistance to being the hero, even a flawed hero.

The advice of authors and friends Cassandra Leoncini, Evonne Agnello, and Karen Reinhart about the publishing process was invaluable.

I benefited from more than a dozen Yellowstone colleagues who checked facts and interpretations in these chapters, but any mistakes are my own. Many friends contributed their time to critiquing the book outline and chapters when they were in very primitive form, including Chip Clark, Claudia Whitman, Lorna Wilkes, Phyllis Mascari, Sara Wiles, and my sister, Becky Strouse.

My husband, Terry Wehrman, never lost faith in the worth of this project, even when it meant that more household chores fell on his shoulders for many years.

The journals of Kathleen O'Leary and Lowell Baltz contributed greatly to the fire chapters. Lowell was a Lake District maintenance worker and fire fighter in 1988, and Kathleen lived at the remote Thorofare Ranger Station with her husband, Ranger Dave Phillips. Many of the statistics in the three fire chapters derive from *Yellowstone's Rebirth by Fire: Rising from the Ashes of the 1988 Wildfires* by Karen Wildung Reinhart (Farcountry Press, Helena, Montana, 2008).

Yellowstone
National Park

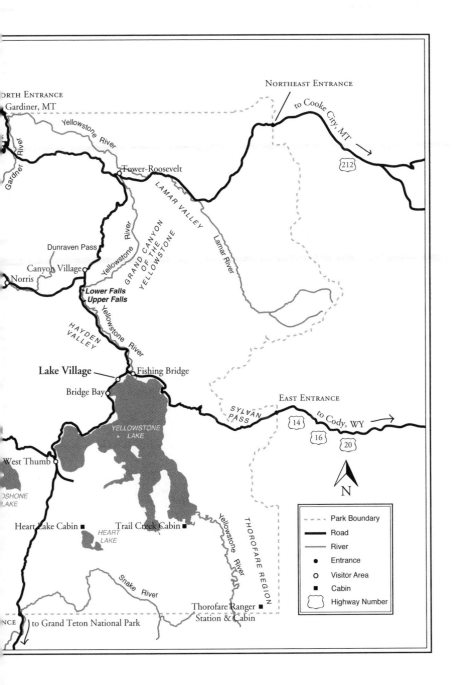

NORTHEAST ENTRANCE

NORTH ENTRANCE
Gardiner, MT

to Cooke City, MT →

Yellowstone River

Gardner River

Tower-Roosevelt

212

LAMAR VALLEY

Dunraven Pass

Yellowstone River

Lamar River

Canyon Village

GRAND CANYON OF THE YELLOWSTONE

Norris

Lower Falls
Upper Falls

Yellowstone River

HAYDEN VALLEY

Lake Village —

Fishing Bridge

EAST ENTRANCE

Bridge Bay

SYLVAN PASS

to Cody, WY →

14

YELLOWSTONE LAKE

16

20

West Thumb

N

SHOSHONE LAKE

Heart Lake Cabin ■

Trail Creek Cabin ■

HEART LAKE

Yellowstone River

THOROFARE REGION

Snake River

Thorofare Ranger ■
Station & Cabin

NCE) to Grand Teton National Park

– – –	Park Boundary
▬▬	Road
▬▬	River
●	Entrance
○	Visitor Area
■	Cabin
⬡	Highway Number

The Real Thing

Here's a poem some guy's written/
'bout Wyoming's sunny skies
'bout her rattlesnakes and wood ticks
Porcupine and bottle flies....

Oh, he sure gives some description
Of this healthy, wealthy state
And he longs to travel back here
so he says at any rate.

But there's one thing that's apparent
I can tell it in his rhyme
This guy must have hit Wyoming
In the good old summer time....

There's sides to this here country
That our poet's never seen,
It would freeze the golden romance
Of any poet's dream.

I'm no pessimist or cynic,
Poet friend, I'd have you know.
But who can dream 'bout romance
When it's thirty-eight below?....

—Tim McCoy (1891-1978)
Western film star who lived in Wyoming most of his life

CHAPTER ONE

Pioneers in Paradise

Let us go then and risk our lives unnecessarily.

—ISAK DINESEN, *OUT OF AFRICA*

*T*HE MOMENT WE HEARD CINDY MERNIN'S VOICE ON THE phone we knew she had bad news. For the past three months we had lived in southwest Colorado, hundreds of miles away from Yellowstone National Park. A day never passed, however, without our thinking about our mountain home. My husband, Terry Wehrman, and I chatted often with our Yellowstone friends to catch up on the latest news about our former human neighbors and the bison, bears, and chickadees. When did the lake freeze? Is there enough snow? After nine years of living year around in the middle of the 2.2-million-acre park, Yellowstone was in our blood. We were Yellowstone. Yellowstone was where our souls lived.

In television documentaries Yellowstone is a magical wonderland in winter. Bison whitened with hoar frost stand silhouetted above the vast, frozen lake. Waterfalls thunder hundreds of feet down through caverns of ice. Geysers hurl steamy droplets high into the winter sky. When we left the park and moved to Man-

cos, Colorado, people in Colorado could hardly believe that anyone was allowed to live in Yellowstone, much less get paid for it.
"Why in the world did you ever leave?"

Yes, it was beautiful, often quiet, a whole other world, we
would tell them. We had also experienced a different Yellowstone,
a Yellowstone with teeth. It was hard to explain something we
only partially understood ourselves. So we learned to smile and
nod and change the subject. In the backs of our minds, we started
to question our mixed feelings about that faraway paradise.

But when Cindy called on January 17, 1994, she reminded us
of Yellowstone's darker side. "Are you sitting down? There's been
an accident on Sylvan Pass." As we tried to deal with the impact
of her call over the following weeks, we pondered our experiences
in the park and their significance.

* * *

In October 1984 Terry received a job offer from the National
Park Service for a winter position at Lake Village. He would be
running a snow groomer, packing the roads for snowmobilers.
Terry was thrilled. Heavy equipment operators like him have a
hard time finding work in Wyoming during the winter. Although
it was a temporary, seasonal position, the pay was good. He looked
forward to working in such a beautiful place, and the prospect of
being isolated did not bother him.

As the owner of the Atlantic City Mercantile and Saloon for
several years in the 1970s, Terry had proven his tolerance for isolation and for an incredible variety of eccentric mountain people.
Atlantic City is an old gold mining town of about fifty people
perched on the Atlantic side of South Pass, a historic route over
the Continental Divide. The "city" is thirty miles from the nearest grocery store, gas station, and post office. Terry had had temporary road jobs before, camping out of the back of a pickup for
weeks at a time, eating his own cooking.

I wasn't so sure. Naturally resistant to change, I had misgivings. Terry and I had been living together for a couple of years, and I did not look forward to the 200-mile separation even though it was just for one winter. There was no question that I would stay in our home in Atlantic City. I had my own work as a freelance writer, and had our dogs to take care of. Furthermore, I had followed a man to his job location once, and it had been a bad decision.

Terry had several years' experience sculpting dirt with scrapers and bulldozers, the heavy equipment used for road construction, so he was qualified for the job. More importantly, he was one of the few applicants willing to spend the winter in Lake Village, a community of twelve employees and spouses in government housing near the north shore of Yellowstone Lake. I would commute to visit him when I could.

We packed what we imagined he might need for his apartment for five months—a mattress, some winter snow gear, canned food, and a lot of books, and delivered it to the apartment assigned to him at Lake Village. The frame fourplex looked more like a motel than the cabin I had pictured in the woods, but its beautiful location made up for that.

We could not delay—the park stopped plowing the roads in the fall, and they would be impassable to anything but snowmobiles by the time Terry's job started in December. While multi-passenger snowcoaches traveled the roads from the more popular entrances, they rarely reached Lake Village. Nobody asked Terry if he had a snowmobile or whether he knew how to operate one. Luckily Terry had snowmobiled half a dozen times. He bought a used Ski-Doo to get through the winter.

When Terry climbed on the Ski-Doo in December and started up the road from the East Entrance, the park was almost unrecognizable. It was not yet open for the winter, so no one else was on the road. Terry had to open the combination lock on the entrance gate to start the thirty-mile journey. Except for the sound of his own snowmobile, the forest was ominously silent, and growing increasingly dark as he climbed up Sylvan Pass and dropped down toward the lake. When he bounced past the Fishing Bridge store—an area bustling with hundreds of visitors and employees during the summer—it was silent, shuttered, and barely visible in the snow. His headlight was the only light he could see as the day faded, and he searched anxiously for the Lake housing area turn off. Finally he saw it, turned up the road, and started his new life.

On my first weekend visit, Terry met me at Pahaska Tepee, a lodge just outside the East Entrance. I was delighted to see him. The snowmobile suit disguised the slender figure I had grown to love, but one could still see that Terry Wehrman was a slender man. He joked that his Indian name would be "Makes No Shadow." Not a slave to the latest fashions, he had worn sideburns and button-down collar shirts when I met him ten years earlier, and he still preferred them, just changed into flannel shirts and sweaters under his snowmobile suit.

I was eager for the new adventure, but snowmobiling was not my idea of fun. I had grown up on skis, downhill skiing during my youth and cross-country skiing for the past fifteen years. Snowmobilers and skiers don't mix. As a skier, I had gagged on the machines' fumes and cringed at their roar. When my fellow skiers and I heard snowmobile riders whining about sore muscles around the fireplace at a snow lodge, we rolled our eyes disdainfully. To visit Terry that winter, I had to swallow my purist pride. Even I had to admit that skiing thirty miles over 8,500-foot-high Sylvan Pass to Lake Village for weekend visits was not an option. The Ski-Doo seat was barely long enough for us to squat on together, even though he made no shadow.

Remembering what we wore on long-distance motorcycle trips in winter, I added a few layers, and I stuffed a few belongings into a knapsack on my back. By the time we had traveled the first two miles from Pahaska to the park entrance, my arm muscles cramped from fighting gravity, trying to hold on to Terry's waist despite the knapsack. As the snowmachine pulled up the slight incline at the park gate, I rolled off the back and into the road at the feet of two rangers and lay there, squirming in the snow, a turtle on its shell.

Not exactly what I would have chosen as my first introduction to our new neighbors. The two rangers, Bob Mahn and Tim Blank, graciously turned their backs and pretended to ignore the scene. Although tempted to laugh, Terry could see two burning dots in the heap of clothing—my eyes glaring at him. (Later, he said I looked like the Michelin man—the rotund figure made of tires—lying there. At the time, however, he was smart enough NOT to mention the Michelin man.)

I pulled my body out of the road and back onto the snowmobile. As we traveled on toward Sylvan Pass, I sublimated my embarrassment into fury at imagined offenses. Terry deliberately swung around corners to try to throw me off; he slammed into the bumps on purpose; he didn't stop often enough for me to stretch my limbs. The steep grade, the light breeze, the heavy pack, my choice of clothes—everything was HIS fault. Squatting on the vibrating, roaring machines, exposed to the elements, was miserable, and I blamed him for putting me there.

Having grown up in Colorado, I was accustomed to high mountain passes. The 300-foot-drop below our trail up Sylvan Pass might not have bothered me if it were not for the huge, orange sign saying, "WARNING! Avalanche zone. No stopping for the next mile. Keep 100 yards between machines." It didn't take much imagination to figure out what that meant: Space the machines so that you won't all get swept off the pass at the same time. The snowmobile road slanted sideways toward the drop off, following the contour of the avalanche chute. Terry yelled at me,

"Lean uphill," hoping that ballast would keep the snowmachine moving forward instead of sliding toward the cliff. I shut my eyes and held on.

After only a few endless minutes, Terry and I rode past the avalanche zone on the pass and started jouncing down the mountain toward Yellowstone Lake. I started to relax and experiment with leaning into the curves, gripping the snowmachine between my thighs. Terry told me to shift my hips rather than tilting my head. Although he was too delicate to mention it, I realized he meant my lower half provided more ballast than my head.

We knew only the basics about motorized over-the-snow vehicles. Both snowmobiles and snowcoaches utilize skis on the front to steer with and tracks to provide momentum. Snowcoaches carry half a dozen passengers in relative comfort inside the heated vehicle, but they took people to Old Faithful, not to Lake. The only option for Lake employees was squatting on a snowmobile, low to the ground, protected only by a windshield. As we traveled toward Lake, I entertained myself with the fantasy of being a pioneer, taking off into the frozen wilderness. Instead of riding a bouncing Conestoga wagon, we bounced on a snow machine; snow coated our world, not dust. Rather than swollen rivers and disease, we had Sylvan and cold.

And buffalo. When we dropped down toward the lakeshore, we encountered the first buffalo. Suddenly there they were, in the road, with no big orange signs instructing us what to do. The first one seemed to fill three-fourths of the road width. Seeing the gigantic beasts filling the road, I had trouble remembering that they were herbivores and presumably would not eat us. Terry pulled over to the side. In the national park, we weren't allowed to ride off the road, so we focused upon making ourselves small and non-threatening.

The first buffalo glanced down at us as he walked past, his eyes glowing red. The smaller one that followed looked younger and more skittish of our roaring, metallic beast. He trotted nervously, daring us to try anything. We didn't. Someone had advised Terry to hide behind the machine if a buffalo charged, but that seemed foolhardy to me. This guy looked ready to lower his head and gore anything in his path, and the snowmachine looked puny as a shield. Coming at us slowly to plan his attack, his horns grew longer and sharper with every step. His hump towered far above his head, blocking out the sun. I considered the power behind that horn if it ripped into my flesh. I wished I hadn't read that gory Hemingway bullfight story earlier in the week.

Terry thought about gunning the machine and leaping over the berm, out of the road. To hell with the rules. But the snow beyond did not look firm enough to support our machine. Maybe we could jump it anyway and climb under the machine when it bogged down in the deep, fluffy snow? The soft snow might cushion us so we wouldn't get crushed by the buffalo's charge.

How many people had died from such encounters, I wondered?

Finally the herd passed by us, Terry squeezed the throttle, and we continued our journey along the lakeshore, over Fishing Bridge, and on to Lake Village. As Terry turned off the key, I sighed with the welcome silence and squirmed with embarrassment about being such a sissy. I remembered an old friend's motto: "You have to scare yourself to death once in awhile to feel really alive."

My thighs felt like a Cossack dancer's after an hour-long performance, and my sore hips barely allowed me to lift my leg over the machine and onto the snow-packed ground. So much for thinking that snowmobiling was a lazy person's sport.

The snowmobile ride over, I silently forgave Terry for his imagined offenses. A real frontier woman would have felt lucky to have such a partner. Terry's heart is as big as all Wyoming. I made an unlikely pioneer woman. Later I would hear stories

from people who lived in the park in the 1930s and on, before
snowmobiles, who were pioneers. I should not have been angry
at Terry. But I was entering a world that had belonged mostly to
men for more than a century—a place where the niche for spouses
and children was still being defined.

Perhaps my fury sprang in part from fear. I had never considered myself especially brave or cowardly. Even though I had
hitchhiked alone across Canada and Europe, I lagged behind
my father and my younger siblings, Becky and Steve, on the ski
slopes, too timid for some of the jumps they leaped off. As a third
generation Colorado native, I was genetically predisposed to living on the fringe of civilization. I was handier with a chain saw
and an ax than with a hair dryer and a curling iron. Terry and I
were both accustomed to mountain living, risk taking, and harsh
winters. A love of adventure first attracted us to one another; we
rode his motorcycle across the country, and he was building a
biplane in his basement when I met him. I was surprised to real-
ize how different Yellowstone was. My first trip suggested new
dimensions for the courage necessary there.

It was a good thing that we were young enough for such a
rigorous life (I was thirty-six and Terry was forty-four.) Looking
at the three other apartments and two houses, I assumed they,
too, must be robust outdoorsmen and women. Turning around,
I could see the Absarokas—the mountains around Sylvan Pass—
glistening on the far side of the lake. An open meadow, begging
for a set of ski tracks, stretched from the apartment toward the
lake. Maybe I could enjoy my weekend visits after all. Little did
I know how many times we would watch that lake freeze and
thaw, listening to its strange moans. How many snowmachines
we would buy for that parking place. What four-legged and two-
legged neighbors we would come to know. Or how many times
Sylvan Pass, the lake, and buffalo would make us feel really alive.

CHAPTER TWO

Flung Together By the Fates

There are two kinds of adventurers: those who really want to have one and those who just as soon not.

—WILLIAM LEAST HEAT MOON, *BLUE HIGHWAYS*

*O*NE EVENING DURING TERRY'S FIRST YEAR IN YELLOWSTONE National Park, Chris and Hume Lilley invited the ten other residents of the Lake community to their home for a chili supper. Hume was Terry's boss, the Lake District maintenance division foreman. He and his wife rented one of the two government houses large enough for everyone to gather. If we had been in the outside world, the women might have been discussing world events or the governor's race or showing pictures of grandchildren. Instead, the topic was snowmobiling. How fast will your John Deere go versus Lorie's Polaris or my Ski-Doo? How do you get around stubborn bison in the road?

For residents of Yellowstone, snowmobiling and watching for wildlife are not mere hobbies. If they wanted to get groceries or go to the dentist or eat a restaurant meal, they had to snowmobile thirty miles over Sylvan Pass to the East Gate or fifty miles to the north. For five months of the year, snowmobiles carried the milk, eggs, hamburger, and any guests brave enough to visit. I listened to Terry's neighbors for ideas to ease my own transition into this new world.

Alice Roller told us she liked to run her snowmobile with the throttle wide open. It infuriated Bob, her cautious husband, especially when he had to rescue her. Maybe that's why she did it. Back in Wisconsin, where she and Bob lived before moving to Yellowstone in 1972, she would zoom across frozen lakes at eighty-five miles per hour with her grandkids on board. Her Yellowstone accidents taught her how risky that could be.

The first time she rolled her machine in Yellowstone, she had been swerving back and forth, trying to entertain herself while she dallied behind her slower husband. When she swerved too wide in Hayden Valley, her machine went off the embankment and Alice flew off, toward the Yellowstone River. To get it back on the road, Bob had to ride his machine into the treacherous, deep snow to pack a track for her, and he never let her forget it. Digging a snowmobile out of deep snow required some physics but lots of mass, and she did not have it. She weighed about one hundred pounds. Looking at her white, curly hair and vivid pink polyester blouse, it was hard for me to imagine the Barney Oldfield racecar driver inside.

The winter before, she accidentally rammed the back of Bob's machine. Traveling home after dark, he had stopped suddenly, trying to avoid hitting a snow-covered buffalo lying in the road. She squeezed her brakes, but snowmobiles don't stop like cars. The brakes stop the track from turning, but then the machines usually slide sideways. They missed hitting the buffalo, bucking and dancing in the headlight's beam ahead of them, but she couldn't avoid hitting Bob's machine.

The next time she rolled her machine, she rolled with it, but she scrambled to her feet and managed to push and pull it upright before Bob came back, looking for her. She hoped to escape another scolding. She could not hide the fact that her windshield had broken off, however.

Although Alice had loved snowmobiling in Wisconsin, after nine winters in Yellowstone, it had lost its appeal. They couldn't choose the weather or the snow conditions when they would go out. By the time I met her, she was sixty years old. The accidents and squatting for thousands of miles had taken their toll; snowmobiling had become a painful ordeal. She still zipped down the road, but when she climbed off the machine, she reached for her crutches. Both of her hips had been reconstructed, and she had knee surgery after one of her snowmobile accidents, but she was determined to stay at Lake with her husband.

She might have lost her spryness but she kept her spunk. When Bob invited her out to lunch on his day off, she didn't hesitate to climb on her machine, knowing the closest lunch would be thirty miles over Sylvan Pass to Pahaska Tepee Lodge, or fifty miles to Old Faithful. One time a blizzard came up while they were enjoying their lunch at Pahaska, and it took them an hour to go half a mile across the top to get back home. Alice would be an invaluable asset to a rookie like me. She hosted dinners, taught me her special techniques for transporting and storing food, and shared tips for dealing with the isolation. "Not everybody can adjust to it. People who party a lot just can't," Bob Roller said. Alice's advice: "Keep your mind and your hands busy."

Young park friends invited her to spend the winter with them on the outside, but the pain kept her up at night, and she didn't want to bother them. I suspected that despite her complaints about Bob, she couldn't stand being separated from him after more than forty years of scrapping. She was sixteen and he was eighteen when they married. They were devoted to each other, but Terry called their relationship complementary antagonism— they kept each other strong. The Rollers had some of their biggest squabbles over snowmobiling. Perhaps the disputes derived from forced dependence. They had been raised in an era of gallantry when men thought they were responsible for protecting the womenfolk. Yellowstone was one of many places where such roles were difficult to maintain.

One fall day, Alice telephoned Bob from inside their trailer to tell him a grizzly was prying the door open. "What do you expect me to do?" he asked, expressing anger instead of the helplessness he felt. Alice was glad to have me as a new audience for her favorite story: She had been busy cooking in their sixty-foot trailer home when she noticed a group of people gathered outside with their cameras. One of them asked, "Did you know there is a grizzly trying to get into your trailer?" When she slid the window open, she found herself face to face with a giant bear. "All I could think of was the mess he could make in the house," she said. Beans baked aromatically in the oven. Salads for the evening's potluck spread across the table. The winter's canned food stores lined the hallways.

She considered hooking a hose to the bathroom faucet and squirting him in the face with hot water, but she realized she didn't have enough time. She kicked at the door to scare him. "He grabbed the bottom of the door with one paw and zip, off it came." When he entered the back door, Alice raced out the front door, leaving it open behind her in the confused hope that the bear would use it rather than exiting through a wall. She ran to the maintenance shop and found Bob. Bob sneaked into the trailer to get his gun from the back bedroom, but a ranger finally appeared and advised Bob not to shoot the bear. Finally the bear was lured out the back door, tranquilized, and sent to live out his days in a Canadian zoo.

Our hostess, Chris Lilley, was nearly twenty years younger than Alice Roller, but she liked snowmobiling even less. She told us her teeth got sore from gritting them as she tried to keep up with Hume on the snowmobiles. Her waist-length hair was as thick and honeyed as her North Carolina accent. She was accustomed to a Southern climate, and she liked cooking, spending time with her children, and collecting stuffed animals. She did not derive pleasure from the out-of-doors and certainly not from snow and buffalo. But Hume had a good job, so they stayed in Yellowstone's interior for nearly ten winters.

During the long Yellowstone winters, Chris's life revolved around the television and the telephone and reading *National Enquirer*. They had the only satellite dish at Lake; anyone else who wanted to watch could connect to their dish, but they had to watch what the Lilleys were watching. To entertain her family back in North Carolina, she mined her life for stories of life in the "wil-l-l-derness" (pronounced with at least five syllables). In her hyperbolic tales, her lifestyle rose from rugged routine to become exotic and hilarious. One time a frozen buffalo chip flew up and hit her in the head. Without a helmet, she would surely have been killed, she said. "If I ran into buffalo like Bob and Alice did, I would have needed an extra bag between my legs."

Once someone at the park headquarters in Mammoth made the mistake of telling Chris how lucky she was to live in the park's interior. Winter residents all believed that Those People (administrators) rarely if ever ventured into the park in the winter. Chris told the visitor what she once said to a doctor giving her a proctology exam. "Why don't you climb up here and see how you like it?" At the chili supper, this story brought roars of approval from the group. Winter exacerbated the normal alienation between any headquarters and its field operations staff, especially during the shoulder season—those months between snowmobile and car seasons when interior residents would sometimes go weeks without any mail.

Terry's neighbors shared stories of Mammoth's insensitivity. Lorie Rippley was shoveling two feet of snow off her car after a long, cold snowmobile ride to Mammoth, when a woman asked her, "Isn't snow wonderful?" Chris's husband, Hume, battled headquarters regularly on their behalf, trying to get regular mail service for them. "Chris and Alice expect mail from their grandchildren," he told them. "When it doesn't come, they feel like someone forgot their birthdays." When the National Park Service tried to convince the Postal Service to deliver mail to the interior, they said it would endanger their employees' life and limb. "Whatever happened to neither snow, nor rain, nor heat, nor gloom of night?" Terry asked.

Chris's favorite snowmobiling topic was buffalo. Soon after my first trip into Yellowstone, I had called the public affairs office to ask about snowmobile v. bison accidents. (Technically, the beasts are bison—there are no buffalo in North America—but that is not what most people call them.) Headquarters reported no record of such encounters. When I mentioned headquarters' comments to Terry's neighbors, they all laughed. "How would they know? They never come out here. No one would report accidents anyway. It would mean too much paperwork."

The park's top bison expert, Mary Meagher, told me that when the park began to groom the roads, the bison numbers expanded exponentially: They could move on the roads without much effort to places with less snow. So in a way, Terry and his fellow groomers were to blame for all the bison in the road. I didn't mention that to Chris, however.

The Rollers shared their own experiences and the legends that circulated around the park interior. One night a snowmobiler knocked on their door in the middle of the night. He had walked in from Hayden Valley, more than ten miles to the north, after he and another guy had crashed into a bison, demolishing the machine and breaking the other guy's arm. The next day in the Hayden Valley, a bison died from a cracked skull.

Everyone at Lake had heard the story about Ranger Tim Blank. One moonless night, he caught sight of some snow-covered sleepy lumps in the road. Grabbing the brakes, his machine missed the first bison but collided with the next. The second bison's horn punctured his windshield and jammed Tim's hand, breaking his wrist. Six inches to the left and the horn would have missed him, but six inches to the right and the horn would have been imbedded in Tim's chest.

A particularly horrifying story featured a guy who careened into a fog bank at night only to find it full of bison. He hit a calf, which flipped through his snowmobile's windshield and into his lap, two of its legs broken. He was sickened by what he had done but even more upset by the reaction of the cows, clearly upset by the calf bawling. The man dove under a log, inches away from their sharp, nervous hooves and close enough to feel their steamy breath. When the bison would start to drift away from him and the calf, he'd jump out and pull the rope, trying to start his snowmobile. Then a new surge of bawling would attract the cows back again. This pattern continued most of the night until he finally realized the accident had pushed in the engine's kill switch. He pulled it back into position and escaped. The calf was not so lucky; it had to be shot.

Alice Siebecker, the ranger who lived at the other end of Terry's quadraplex, said she found a new way to scare bison off the road. Even the biggest ones scattered when she alternatively accelerated and decelerated, waved her arms, and made other sharp motions to scare them. During such parties, Chris could laugh at the absurdities of our lives. Yet she brooded about the dangers during the long winter days she spent alone. The bison on the road worried most of us, but they terrified Chris. In addition, Chris suffered from asthma; one of her closest friends died in Yellowstone one summer from the same condition. Would she be next?

Of course I thought skiing would save everyone from the winter doldrums. When I tried to nudge Chris outside one day to ski, she said she doesn't go out "in weather like this." Looking out at the sunshine and the snow melting from the roof, I realized she really was more content inside baking cakes and cookies, and making fudge for Christmas. Women like her created these holiday traditions that drove us career women crazy if we tried to uphold them. Nevertheless, we all relished the extravagant desserts she prepared for our potlucks.

Before going home from our chili dinner, we crowded around the Lilleys' VCR and watched *Yellowstone in Winter*. The movie on Nature showed all the animals and one young, robust human family living at Canyon Village, Steve and Angela and their children. In the show, it looked as if the winterkeeper there at Canyon was the only person who shoveled snow from the roofs in Yellowstone to keep them from collapsing. We all looked at Lorie Rippley, twenty-three, her lacy white blouse contrasting so nicely with her tan face. She was tan in December for a reason—she shoveled the government roofs in the Lake area. The film didn't mention Lorie or her counterparts in other areas of the park. Lorie laughed, saying, "I'll have to call Steve and get him over here to take care of our roofs." The film didn't depict Alice Roller with her aching joints or Chris Lilley with her fears and lively stories. The rest of the human community in the heart of Yellowstone seemed invisible.

Looking around the room, I remembered visiting a church in the Denver ghetto where a woman fell suddenly to the floor, speaking in tongues. The preacher said, "Leave her lay where Jesus flang her." Here in Yellowstone, the fates had flung a bunch of people together, only some of whom would have chosen it on their own.

CHAPTER THREE
Making Peace with Paradise

When you change the way you look at things, the things you look at change.

—WAYNE DYER

*S*NOW GOSSIPED SHAMELESSLY AT LAKE WITHOUT MUCH wind or melting to hush it up. Two little trenches in the trail showed where Lorie had dragged her ladder behind her snow-machine on her way to shovel roofs. With only twelve people at Lake, I knew that Bill Berg (a winterkeeper for TW Services at the Lake Lodge) had made the new ski tracks up Elephant Back ridge. When I attempted the steep ski run down the side of the buried water reservoir, I knew Bob Roller could see my sitzmark and judge my skiing prowess when he checked the reservoir the next day.

Our lives established a pattern. Terry worked nine hours a day grooming the roads in the Lake District, which meant he had long weekends every other week. So on his long weekends I found a dog sitter and drove from Atlantic City, Wyoming, to the Yellowstone National Park gate to visit him for a few days. As we climbed off the snowmobile, we made a ritual of looking across the lake to greet Mount Doane (a 10,500-foot peak named for one of Yellowstone's early explorers). This soon became "our mountain." During the days that Terry worked, I sat at the typewriter until late afternoon, when I started to explore the area on skis.

Once on skis, I began to make friends with Yellowstone, which seemed much more hospitable than it did from the back of a snowmobile. I had practically grown up on skis, spending every winter weekend and Christmas vacation downhill skiing with my family since I was nine years old. As an adult, I had switched to cross-country skiing. From the beginning, the patterns of our lives revolved around our powerful, influential neighbor, Yellowstone Lake. As a skier, I was not limited to traveling on the road. I gravitated toward the patch of open water below Fishing Bridge, a mile-and-a-half ski from Terry's home. Each afternoon, I read the animal tracks in the snow instead of a newspaper to discover the news of the day. On her regular rounds, a coyote used my ski tracks to avoid having to make her own path through the deep snow, and mouse tracks overlaid hers. Sometimes I'd see a small, round hole—evidence of the most furtive night hunter, the ermine, diving into the snow for a vole.

In most parts of Wyoming, especially Atlantic City, the wind crust on the snow facilitated travel for skiers and small animals. At Lake there was neither enough wind nor enough warming to consolidate the snow in December. Rather than packing my own trail through the deep, soft snow, I often followed bison tracks. As they sought grass, the bison left a network of trenches and wide places where they fed, swinging their heads back and forth to plow the snow down to ground level. I learned to ski in these thigh-deep trenches.

If the bison had far to go, they chose the roads, their hooves imprinting a pattern over the grooves left by Terry's grooming machine. We had a mutual aid society there at Lake because it was so hard for the four-legged creatures to make a living—the coyote and I relied upon the bison tracks and the bison upon the groomer's. Only the mice could travel freely across the meadows, leaving nothing more than a snowflake's track across the surface, dotted with stacks of chaff dropped from the grasses they had nibbled.

Each morning before dawn as his groomer trundled down the road, Terry listened to the KNX radio announcer in Los Angeles, the signal skipping off the atmosphere to the middle of Yellowstone a thousand miles away: "Avoid the northbound lane of the Santa Ana Freeway. Traffic is backed up for half a mile due to construction....An accident has stopped all westbound traffic on the Santa Monica Freeway. Find another route." Terry smiled at the contrast on his roadway. His headlights illumined only bison tracks breaking the surface of the newly fallen snow.

The more Terry learned about his work, the more it excited his love of new challenges.

Snowmobilers and snowcoaches used some of the same roads in winter as cars used in the summer in Yellowstone. The park groomers prepared the roads for snowmobilers by flattening the drifts, smoothing the ruts, and sometimes reconstructing roadways after avalanches or blizzards. Without grooming, snowmobiling would be impossible for anyone but the experts. The groomers in each district operated machinery much like what was used on ski slopes—a tractor unit with a heated cab. The Lake District's was manufactured by the Delorian Motor Company (DMC). It had a fourteen-foot-wide plow blade on the front and a barrel-shaped, grooved drum on the back. The tractor crawled on tracks, pushing the snowplow blades out in front. The blades contoured the snow while the tracks and drum packed it so that even inexperienced snowmobilers would not get stuck. Terry's territory included the road over Sylvan Pass to the east as well as the road north to Mud Volcano and the southwest road to Pumice Point (half way to West Thumb).

Several park districts utilized the DMC snow groomer with a fourteen-foot-wide plow blade on the front and a barrel-shaped, grooved drum on the back. The tractor crawled on tracks, pushing the snowplow blades that contoured the snow, while the following tracks and drum packed it. (NPS file photo by Jim Peaco)

While grooming the roads north to Mud Volcano and southwest to Pumice Point took less time, he liked the long, ten-hour run over Sylvan Pass for two reasons: the challenges presented by Sylvan Pass and the opportunity to join Ranger Bob Mahn for lunch outside the East Entrance. They ate at Pahaska Tepee, the restaurant near the old lodge built by Buffalo Bill. When I wasn't visiting, Terry grew tired of his own cooking seven days a week, and the East Gate ranger was good company.

The solitary work suited Terry, moving through the wild country alone, able to concentrate on his own work rather than upon supervising other employees. "Can you believe I get paid to do this?" he would say when he got home. While the snow groomer differed from other equipment he had run in road construction, it used many of the same skills—the eye for contours, the touch for operating the controls, and the satisfaction of a job well done. While the slow pace of the groomer—seven miles per hour—would have driven another operator mad, Terry enjoyed watching the scenery and the wildlife while he worked. His schedule varied, depending upon the amount of traffic and whether it snowed. Dozens of snowmobilers pounding down a road would create a washboard that shook riders unmercifully.

Unlike the traffic reports he listened to from LA, heavy traffic for Terry meant bison jousting to improve their positions. As he studied the bison dynamics, he learned that each cow and calf seemed to be assigned a place in the procession. When the groomer disrupted them, some would try to move toward the front, but the others quickly nudged or butted them back into their proper order again. The mature bulls traveled apart from the cows and calves during the winter. The growling, giant grooming machine intimidated even the biggest, 2,000-pound bull. One day he watched one dive off the groomed road, sink almost out of sight, and topple on to his nose. Then he gathered his feet under him for galloping leaps, just as our golden retriever dog, Sarge, did in very deep snow. Effective, but expensive in energy expenditures.

Occasionally visitors came around a curve and saw, to their alarm, several bison charging toward them ahead of the groomer. The bison could move slightly faster than the groomer's seven miles an hour. Terry had no intentions of herding the bison toward the panicked visitors, but his options were limited to the road. To avoid the deep snow, the bison stayed in the road, sometimes for several miles. When such an impasse developed, Terry usually stopped the groomer, hoping experienced snowmobilers would crowd up on the bison and pass them in the other lane. If the visitors were too terrified to move, Terry would motion them to the right side of the road and then inch the groomer forward to get the bison moving past the unhappy tourists.

One expert estimated that the total number of bison in the park increased from 2,000 to 3,000 because of grooming. Winter was no longer the predator that kept their numbers down, and they lacked any other predators. Grizzlies rarely attacked a full-grown bison unless it was injured or sick, and wolves had not yet been reintroduced in the park.

On the days that Terry groomed the road along the lakeshore toward West Thumb, he saw fewer bison than on the east road. If he was lucky, he might spot river otters near Pumice Point, where thermal waters kept holes open in the ice. One sub-zero day he and Alice Siebecker watched the otters dive and surface, slithering over one another's bodies like a mess of snakes. Alice had been patrolling the roads for speeders and for snowmobilers in trouble. A ranger naturalist before she took her law enforcement training, Alice told him the otters traveled under the ice for miles, knowing where the air holes were. They played around the edges of the holes to keep them from freezing over. Biologists might argue that the otters were working hard, diving into the icy waters to catch fish, lugging cutthroat trout a third their weight to the surface, and occasionally fending off a coyote that tried to snatch their food. To most onlookers, they just looked like fun-loving clowns. After weeks of watching their antics, Terry decided that when he died, he wanted to come back as an otter in Yellowstone.

At Lake, I usually skied alone. In the civilized world if I sought the euphoria of natural body chemicals, I would have been pounding my way through sweaty traffic at the health club. In Yellowstone, I produced my endorphins in the snow, threading my way through the bison tracks. Snowmobilers occasionally zoomed by on the road, but there were no public facilities open during the winter within thirty miles of Lake, so the traffic usually dwindled to nothing by late afternoon. Without the constant whine and rattle of civilization, I tuned in to the whispers of dramas outside, both comic and tragic, the stage constantly changing with the temperatures and the angle of the sun.

One afternoon I read a one-act play scrawled in the snow. An owl dived and struck just hard enough for his head and feet to reach eight inches below the surface. The owl must have heard a mouse under the snow. His tail and wing feathers each left their imprint on top. Such grace. If I tried that, the snow would be completely trashed by my thrashing, if not by the wreckage itself.

Often the crunch of my skis and the puffs of my breaths were the only sounds. Climbing the bluff above Fishing Bridge each evening, I learned to hold my breath to listen to the swans, sometimes feeling faint before I remembered to exhale. Looking out over the lake for signs of freezing, it was hard to imagine such a large body of water ever becoming solid. But the next Ice Age hovered at my elbow. The lake remained frozen over for nearly half the year, usually not thawing until late May or early June. The oldtimers told tales about haunting sounds from the lake's ice, so we awaited the freezing eagerly.

The lake itself was larger than many entire national parks—132 square miles. If there were a road around it, the road would be 142 miles long, but of course there was no road. In fact, road travelers could tour only one-fifth of its circumference. The rest was in the wilderness. Because of its immense size, it influenced the weather thirty miles away, on the other side of Sylvan Pass. Bob Mahn, the East Gate ranger, told us that until the lake froze each year, the East Entrance received rain and snow that either equaled or surpassed what we received at Lake. After the freeze, it was less.

The lake stretched twenty miles across from our shoreline to the end of the southeast arm. Beneath her surface she hid many of the familiar Yellowstone features—geysers, fumaroles, and 400-foot-deep canyons. Far below the reach of sunbeams, strange wildlife dwelled, living on thermal chemicals instead of photosynthesis.

One evening I was packing a new trail on a bluff above the Yellowstone Lake outlet when I heard the DMC groomer rolling back from Sylvan Pass. My heart leaped in anticipation of seeing

Terry. Changing my course to intersect his, I studied the slope off the bluff and toward the outlet at Fishing Bridge. Although the snow was deep, I figured I could point my skis straight down and gravity would propel me down the nearly vertical embankment. Wrong. The skis sank and I tumbled over them, hanging upside down from my bindings. Since even my poles couldn't reach any solid ground, I tried to throw my legs over my head to get my skis below me. They wouldn't move. As I hung there, I imagined Terry rolling by without even seeing me in the dying light. Only the white undersides of my skis were exposed, and I was still a quarter mile from the road.

When I finally unburied myself and proceeded a few feet, I saw a bison ahead. Not willing to crawl back up that hill, I told him, "I won't bother you, if you don't bother me." Verbal reasoning may not have been his forte, but fortunately he wasn't inclined to move more than necessary through the deep stuff. Hurriedly circling around him, I arrived at the lakeside below the bridge just as Terry passed over it. When I waved, he blinked his lights and rumbled homeward, knowing I was out for fun and not looking for a ride.

Occasionally Terry or one of my neighbors—Alice Siebecker or Lorie Rippley—would join me skiing on the weekend. They worked long days for the National Park Service, mostly outside, leaving home and returning in the dark during December, when the mercury seldom moved above zero. Gradually, we became better acquainted during our afternoon skis. Lorie lived next door to Terry. When I met her, she looked like an athlete who worked out every day, and in fact she did—worked out with a shovel. Her impish smile caused one to wonder what trouble she had up her jacket sleeve. Her active mind and profane language made me laugh. (My mother learned to swear working for the Red Cross during World War II, so I was not put off by it.) Although Alice spent much of the day on a snowmobile, she was also strong and athletic with a ready smile that no doubt disarmed angry speeders when she pulled them over. When she accompanied me on ski jaunts, she helped me to recognize the dried stalk sticking out of the snow as the fireweed that glowed pink in the summer, and she explained the different owl calls that we heard at night.

As Christmas approached, Terry realized he had to work and could not leave the area. Yellowstone attracted lots of visitors over the Christmas break, and he had to do his part to keep the roads in good shape for them. Christmas was always a family time for us, and we wanted to share our once-in-a-lifetime Yellowstone opportunity, so we had rashly invited seven family members and friends to join us for Christmas. We didn't ask any of our new acquaintances at Lake for advice, or they might have told us why they never tried such a thing. Not only did we need to come up with enough blankets, pillows, food, and floor space, we also had to provide snowmobiles, helmets, and snow gear for everyone.

Terry's neighbors pitched in to help, and we finally found enough snowmobiles to bring in Terry's teenaged children (Sheri and Scott, who lived in California) and my folks (Ed and Sue Ambler, who lived in Riverton, Wyoming). Our friend Lorna Wilkes and her children, Erin and Jason, from Evanston, Wyoming, took the snowcoach to West Thumb, and we rode twenty-one miles to pick them up on our snowmobiles. We borrowed a sled to haul in a turkey and enough other food to feed nine people three meals a day for several days.

When our first four visitors arrived at the East Entrance, Sylvan Pass acted like her usual, inhospitable self. Storms had nearly obliterated the trail; there was only about thirty feet visibility; and thus the entrance was closed to the public. However, we were all determined to proceed with our plans. Terry took his sixteen-year old daughter on his machine, and I put Scott, fourteen, on the back of my snowmobile for the trip in.

Dad, then sixty-four years old, and Sue, fifty-nine, rented

a snowmobile at Pahaska Tepee. Dad and Sue were hardy out-door people who had snowmobiled before (once) so they didn't hesitate to sign up for an adventure. Dad's hands were cold so he asked Susie to drive. When they saw the sign that said, "Ava-lanche Danger next 100 yards," fear struck their hearts, just as it had mine. In fact, the conditions were worse than my first trip into Yellowstone, much worse than any of us anticipated. Susie said, "What do I do, Ed?" "Kick it in the ass," he advised her from the backseat, knowing that dawdling was not wise under those conditions. Since they had married ten years earlier, Susie had ac-companied Dad on various hair-raising adventures. With typical true grit, Susie gripped the throttle tighter and raced to keep up with the rest of us.

Once we arrived at Lake, it all seemed worth it. Seeing Yel-lowstone through our guests' eyes made us appreciate our good fortune even more. "Snow" spoken through the lips of a fourteen-year-old California boy is a prayer. Fascinated by the white stuff we took for granted, Scott wanted a real blizzard. Picking up a handful of the dry, cold granules, he squinted his eyes shut to savor the experience, saying it felt kind of hot until he gripped it tightly in his palm for a moment. When the snow fell lightly, flake by flake, it reminded him of dandelions gone to seed.

Watching animals was, of course, the favorite part of their visit. We knew we could promise them bison and probably trum-peter swans. We loved the swans and couldn't imagine killing them to make quill pens, as was commonly done in many places during the 1600s to 1800s. We hoped our guests would also get to see otters and coyotes during their brief stay. They shared our wariness about the bison when we encountered them while snow-mobiling, but when we went out on skis, they soon realized they did not need to worry about the animals too much. On the road-ways, park regulations confined man and beast to the narrow cor-ridor together. With the wide, open meadows, we all had plenty of room to avoid one another. I shared the advice given by one of our more experienced neighbors about body language—if a bison raises its tail, it is either going to charge or discharge. A tossing head also indicates that a bison is unhappy.

Standing together a few feet in front of one big bull, Lorna and I could not see over his hump, which was more than five feet high. We watched his black, narrow tongue flick out one side of his mouth and then the other as he chewed his cud and licked his lips. We felt more like giggling than retreating. To conserve energy, he moved so-o-o s l o w l y, like a mechanized museum animal, whose creator thought the neck could never possibly hold the massive head if the movement were too quick. I read later that the muscles holding the head hooked onto the bones at the top of the hump, which acted as a crane holding up the head. Bison that lived in areas with deep snow like Yellowstone developed bigger humps over the decades.

When we went out skiing, we tried to estimate the temperatures from the sound of the snow. Most days it squeaked because the temperature was usually below 14° Fahrenheit. The scientists say this is mostly because it lacks water to lubricate the ice crystals. One sub-zero afternoon, the snow spraying behind our skis tinkled like chandelier prisms shattering. When the wind blew, the pines whined and squealed eerily, as if they might fall at any moment.

Skiing up Elephant Back ridge early one morning, we depended upon the teenage boys' competitiveness to break the trail for the rest of us. When we paused for a break on the steep trail, ice crystals shimmered against the dark forest. Jason, the most daring skier of our group, could not resist diving off into deep, steep, untracked powder snow. He paid for it later, slugging his way back up to the trail.

Approaching Fishing Bridge one day on our cross-country skis, we lingered on the lookout point above the outlet, savoring the sight of the partially frozen lake against the backdrop of the Absaroka Mountains. Sensing our presence, the golden-eye ducks spun away from the water, their wings whistling their alarm. When we got closer, we heard a sharp bark just as we spied a bald eagle approaching. I wasn't sure what made the sound until we saw three otters swimming just beyond the ice. One of them must have sounded a warning about the eagle.

We had no television, but the four teenagers did not miss it. The boys constructed a little ski jump and practiced well after dark using the yard light. We sang Christmas carols at our neighbors' doors, decorated our tree, and topped it with a star that Jason fashioned out of cardboard and aluminum foil. On Christmas Eve we went over to our neighbor Lorie's house for pizza and then watched the teenagers (Scott, Sheri, Jason, and Erin) break dance around the tree. They taught us adults the "Santa Rap."

On Christmas Day, we chattered noisily as we skied toward Fishing Bridge until we spotted trumpeter swans on the shore below. Even without knowing that they had been brought back from the brink of extinction, Susie and Lorna were stunned by their size and majesty. Scolding, the swans lined up, slid into the black water, and glided along the shore, their elegant necks stretched alertly.

From the time the swans arrived from Canada in October until late winter, the big, white birds were messengers, always having something to say. Such a noisy bunch in the snow-muted silence. At first we imagined a gaggle of fifth-grade clarinetists. Or those paper horns that roll out on New Year's Eve. No, Terry said, not that irritating. The park bird biologist Terry McEneaney compared the sound to the honking of a Hong Kong taxicab. Talk about irritating. I read somewhere that an Indian tribe called the trumpeter "ko-hoh," but the article did not identify which tribe. Ko-hoh is close to their call, if pronounced with a slightly nasal twang.

Several swans took off, churning a long runway and then cir-cling. Leaning back, we heard the slow, rhythmic swoosh of their giant wings as they crossed over our heads. Each wing could have covered a person from head to toe. Seven. Seven swans beating across the sky, the edges of their bodies outlined in silver from the low Christmas sun—a good omen for the coming year.

CHAPTER FOUR
Breaking the Ice

You were glad in a way to see the plows come because you wanted to get fresh groceries and stuff. But you were always glad to see the gates close in the fall, too.

—JERRY BATESON, LAKE WINTERKEEPER 1950-1975

*W*HEN BILL BERG CALLED TERRY AND EVERYONE ELSE IN the Lake community one day in March, I was lucky enough to be visiting. I would not have wanted to miss the big event of the spring season. "Come down to Lake Hotel at 3 P.M. Saturday. We're knocking the snow off the roof."

Bill Berg and Gary Durfey were the winterkeepers for TW Services, the park concessionaire that ran the hotels and lodges at the time. Like Lorie, they were responsible for keeping roofs cleared of snow so they would not collapse, but they took care of the concessionaire's buildings while Lorie and her partner shoveled the government buildings. Bill and Gary spent every day using giant saws and shovels to remove snow from the ancillary buildings. A few times a year, however, they pulled the cable on the hotel.

By March of that year, several feet of snow had accumulated

on Lake Hotel, an elegant three-story, frame building first built in 1891. Winds blew snow across the frozen lake and across the tops of Lake Hotel and Lake Lodge, where it drifted on the roofs. Early in the season, the winterkeepers strung a heavy-duty cable across the ridge of the hotel. One end was secure while the other end could be released with a sharp tug. The high angle of the roof promised a big load of snow but only if the temperature, depth, and conditions were right.

By the appointed time, nine spectators, including two children and two dogs, had gathered via skis and snowmobiles. Wearing crampons, Gary climbed up on the steep roof and released one end of the cable so Bill could pull it from below. Bill wore snowshoes, hoping for a quick getaway. The ice and snow could be deadly when it hit the ground and shattered. The rough cable (designed for opening garage doors) cut below the snow. At first, only a few chunks fell, and the crowd was disappointed. Then suddenly a key anchor point was cut. An avalanche cracked free from the roof's peak, thundering down the roof and dropping thirty feet to the ground. After a glance to be sure that Bill and the dogs had escaped, the crowd responded with appreciative applause. The event had surpassed its billing.

The next day, Alice Roller invited the winterkeepers and the Park Service employees and their families over for dinner. Wherever I had lived, I had hosted potlucks so everyone could share in the cooking. Alice, however, insisted on cooking the whole meal for everyone. After dinner, the conversation turned to Terry's big news. He had been hired as a permanent employee. This was not going to be a one-winter detour for a seasonal job after all. He was going to live at Lake and be responsible for taking care of the roads in the Lake District year around, grooming in the winter, plowing in the spring and fall, and supervising a road-maintenance crew in the summer.

Everyone was amazed. Seasonal workers often had to wait

years for permanent positions. Terry told them he just got lucky—he was at the right place at the right time. The people around the table appreciated the new guy's humility and knew this explanation was partially true. When it first opened up as a permanent position the previous fall, no one had applied. Apparently no one else would consider such an isolated location, or perhaps their wives vetoed the idea. However, I knew it was more than luck. Terry had slaved over his application for several days, writing down every job he had ever held and the skills he learned from it. In the private construction world, heavy equipment operators typically worked one or two different jobs a year, and he had been doing that for ten years. He also was awarded points for serving in the Air Force during the Vietnam War.

I shared Terry's excitement about the position, but I confessed to the people around the table that I couldn't help feeling anxious about Sylvan Pass. On our latest trip from the East Entrance, Sylvan had acted particularly cantankerous. Thanks to Bob Mahn, we had arrived safely, but the trip had ended badly for our sled full of food. The fierce wind at the top of the pass had blown snow over the road, leaving a steep side slope slanting toward the cliff. Visitors were stranded on both sides of the pass. We waited with other travelers on the east side while Ranger Bob Mahn expertly negotiated the difficult terrain, riding his snowmobile back and forth several times to make a track across the mile-long avalanche zone.

The other five snowmobilers waiting near us lived in Powell, Wyoming. They had been snowmobiling in Yellowstone since the early 1970s—before the Park Service began grooming the roads—so they had to be good. Nevertheless, they had appreciated Bob's efforts to clear a track and make their travel easier. More than six feet tall and 250 pounds, Bob was a bear of a man who thrived up there among the 10,000-foot high Absarokas. When he climbed on his snowmachine, it looked like he had borrowed a child's tricycle from one of his neighbors.

To them, he was "Bob," not "The Ranger." Often people in border towns near national parks resent the National Park Service and all its rules. But the people in that far corner of Wyoming knew Bob and liked him. He participated in the local community, belonging to the Powell Antique Car Club and serving as a volunteer EMT during the seasons when the roads to his NPS home were open and he could get out for calls. I liked Bob, too, partly because he had never mentioned my inglorious first entry into the park when I had fallen off the snowmobile at his feet.

When Bob returned to our group, he yanked off his helmet and stocking cap and stood there in the howling wind, grinning, his cheeks rosy from the exertion and the wind, his thick dark beard bristling with enthusiasm. Bob said we should have no problem. His slow, deep voice was reassuring so we took our place in line to cross. After frequent encounters with Sylvan and other hazards, Terry often tried to take the edge off our anxiety by grinning and saying, "Another A&W Adventure!" playing on the letters of our last names, Ambler and Wehrman.

The top looked better after Bob's work but certainly not easy to us, a couple of rookies with old machines and a bulky sled. My attitude had improved since my first trip into Yellowstone. We had learned snowmobiling did not have to be so uncomfortable; we didn't dress to the extent of immobility; and we tied the pack onto the machine or sled. Whenever possible we took separate machines instead of riding double. On Sylvan that day I realized that we were not going to die; the only danger was getting stuck, and if we did, it was up to the guys to get us unstuck. Terry took off with the lighter-weight Ski-Doo pulling the sled full of groceries. After he got across the worst part, I closed my face shield and climbed on to our 440 Rupp American machine. We were the only people at Lake with such an old machine. Popular in its day, the Rupp was known for being fast, stable, and heavy. As instructed, I perched on the Rupp's up-slope running board (instead of sitting on the seat) so that my weight would keep it from sliding out of the track and toward the cliff below. It was the first time in my life I wished I were heavier.

Suddenly one ski drifted out of the track and the Rupp dove into the deep snow, slamming to a stop, hopelessly stuck. Terry post holed back to my side, and we stomped a platform for ourselves below the Rupp. Combining our full strength, we tried to bench press it back into the track above. The heavy S.O.B. barely budged. Then Bob came to help. He grabbed the Rupp and tossed it onto the track as if he were lifting an empty box, and we understood why he thought we would have no problem. He waved cheerily as we took off toward Terry's home.

When we arrived at Lake, we pulled back the tarp over the sled with trepidation. Terry, aka Mr. Over-Prepared, always carried a can of gasoline, just in case we ran out. The rough ride had burst the plastic gallon of milk, and the milk swirled around in the bottom of the sled with spilled gasoline. The smelly mixture had soaked through all the cardboard boxes of food. At least the canned goods survived so we had something to eat.

When we told our story to the group gathered at the Rollers' house, the veteran food hoarders laughed sympathetically and added their own stories and advice about protecting their winter supplies of food. After an especially bumpy trip back to Lake, Alice Siebecker noticed people staring incredulously at her. The Roma tomatoes she had packed had mashed into a pulp that oozed out the back of her grocery box, leaving a bloody trail behind her.

Bob and Alice Roller had learned the hard way to call the grocery store ahead of time and ask someone to freeze milk before they arrived. They had tried to bring milk in a suitcase, packed with their clothes. "We learned you couldn't do that." It rode better as a solid, and when they thawed it at home, they shook it hard to re-mix it. Don't pack pizza on its side, or all the ingredients will vibrate off. Put a rubber band around egg cartons with some padding inside. Pack in boxes, preferably with lids. If the weather is twenty degrees Fahrenheit or less, pack the bananas and avocadoes inside your snowmachine suit and the lettuce in a cooler to keep them from freezing. One man bought frozen bread dough after too many attempts to pull triangular bread slices back into squares. Want to avoid bursting milk containers? One of our neighbors innocently reported buying Bailey's Irish Cream for his morning coffee.

Someone at the table started telling stories about Bob Mahn and his legendary strength. Once in 1976 when he was working at Lake, the rangers received a call about two rowdy drunks fighting at the Lake Hotel Bar. Normally a ranger would have waited for reinforcements, but Bob waded into the melee. Both men were rolling around on the floor. Bob pulled the top man off, took him to the floor, and was handcuffing him when the second man jumped on Bob's back. Just as the backup rangers burst through the swinging doors, Bob reached up with his free arm, gripped the second man, and tossed the drunk over his shoulder onto the floor. The fight was over. The other rangers admonished Bob, saying he should have waited for backup. Bob said, "Ah, no, they were more of a nuisance than anything."

Bob loved to eat. Although much of his bulk was muscle, he worried frequently about his weight. Sometimes when Terry and Bob went to Pahaska Tepee for lunch, Bob would just order coffee. As they talked, he would hover like a vulture over Terry's food, watching each morsel pass from the plate to Terry's mouth. Terry feared that one day Bob's self-control would dissolve, and he would leap across the table to attack Terry's hamburger.

When they had lunch together, Terry and Bob talked about how Sylvan kept their jobs interesting, which made me think of the old Chinese curse: "May your life be interesting." I was morbidly preoccupied with the danger when Terry was up there alone. My fear was partially irrational: In the movies, any couple as happy and as much in love was destined for tragedy. Listening to the world news—boat hijackings, plane crashes, executions of South Africans, bombings—disaster seemed destined to touch our lives sooner or later. But my fears were also fueled by what I had seen of Sylvan and the stories I had heard. No one took the pass for granted.

Lorie often had to snowmobile over Sylvan alone for her job. She was my mentor. I had lived alone or with female roommates for most of my adult life. Despite my independence outside the park, however, I did not dare to snowmobile long distances alone yet. I didn't have a park radio, and our snowmachines were unreliable. The dependence embarrassed me. I had read about Colette Dowling's book, *The Cinderella Complex: Women's Hidden Fear of Independence.* She said some women had an unconscious desire to be taken care of by others. Surely that could not apply to me. Lorie gave me hope that I, too, could learn to travel safely without my husband between civilization and Yellowstone.

Spring comes to the park subtly at first. When Terry escorted me out after my weeklong visit, we saw a single cloud formed by the earth's hot breath at Steamboat Point float west across the lake—much different than the fog of ice crystals we were accustomed to near the lake. Nevertheless, snow continued to fall, and everyone was tired of winter. Near Mary Bay, the bison had wearied of winter, too. Seeking new feeding grounds, they trudged down the road, conserving energy. Although they occasionally still bumped heads with one another in irritation, they seemed too tired to follow through. Not everything survived the winter. On our way out, we saw a bison carcass beside the road. When Terry returned a few hours later, he noticed the carcass moving. As he passed, a coyote emerged from inside the carcass, smeared red and licking his lips.

Mary Bay and the rest of the lake were still covered with ice.

At an elevation of 7,700 feet, Yellowstone Lake ice would not melt from solar energy until May or June. The park had used dynamite to break up the ice floes at the outlet and around the boat docks as recently as the 1960s. We were told it was to protect the historic Fishing Bridge and boat docks, but I suspected they just wanted to speed the arrival of spring. In the 1920s, the explosives were necessary. Yellowstone did not have any motorized road equipment to clear the snow or ice. In 1986 we visited Horace Albright, who had been Yellowstone's superintendent from 1919 to 1929. He told us he acquired two railroad carloads of TNT left over from World War I. Each fall, he had his men cache some of it at places where the snow would be the deepest, so they wouldn't have to haul in the explosives on snowshoes. In the spring, they would blast the roads open.

In April, Terry called me in Atlantic City and said he needed to get out of the park. He hungered for the smell of something besides diesel fumes and bison. He suffered from sensory deprivation from all those months of seeing only white and forest green, and the twittering of newly arrived swallows and sparrows made his blood race with the restless fever of the season. He knew spring had arrived in the outside world but it hadn't yet reached Yellowstone. The park service had started plowing roads in other districts, but it would take weeks for them to reach Lake. So we agreed to meet in Thermopolis, Wyoming, part way between Yellowstone and Atlantic City. On his drive from Cody to Thermopolis, Terry saw that spring had indeed arrived outside the park. Tiny calves and lambs kicked and chased one another in the greening grass.

As we strolled along the Big Horn River, we relished the red earth and the damp, spring smells and talked about how our lives were about to change. With his permanent job, I would move to Lake, but what would we do about Scott and Sheri? Terry's children had been spending every summer with him in Atlantic

City since his divorce thirteen years earlier. They loved Atlantic City and wouldn't be happy about the change. What would we do about our separate bank accounts? The 100-year-old log cabin that I rented in Atlantic City? The house that he had built there?

Flush with the excitement of a salary and benefits, Terry offered to support me after we married while I wrote the book I was working on. Immersed in the details and missing the big picture, I babbled about the inadvisability of joint back accounts and how we both liked our independence, etc. etc. etc. Trusting myself and the fates had always been easier for me than trusting another person, especially a man. At dinner that night in Thermopolis, my mind wandered back over our conversation, especially the "after we are married" part. "Did you propose to me?" Indeed, he had.

Chapter Five

Another A&W Adventure

*It is going where the two of you—and marriage, time, life, history,
and the world—will take it. You do not know the road; you have
committed your life to a way.*
—Wendell Berry in "Poetry and Marriage: The Use of
Old Forms"

THE FOLLOWING MONTHS RACED BY IN A FLURRY OF transitions. Yellowstone was unrecognizable in the summer, and we had to learn to deal with the hordes of summer rather than the hoards of winter. Many Wyoming residents avoid the park completely during the summer because traffic backs up behind "bison jams," "moose jams," and "bear jams," and it takes much longer to drive park roads during the heat of the summer than to snowmobile the same distances in the winter.

Terry felt as if he had moved to the city, but actually the city had come to him. Hundreds of employees arrived to serve as busboys, waiters, store clerks, mechanics, medical clinic doctors, plumbers, gas station attendants, law enforcement rangers, campground attendants, and interpretive rangers. Millions of visitors drove through each summer. With them came all the city's amenities and problems. Unlike winter, we could buy a loaf of bread or a sandwich at the Hamilton Store or sip wine and listen to the string quartet at Lake Hotel. For entertainment, we could attend ranger programs to learn more about the stars and the mud pots, meet at the employee pub for pizza, or drive to Mary Bay to look for a grizzly.

Our friends and family could visit us without worrying about snowmobiles and winter gear. Terry's teenaged children could live with us during the summer, and despite their resistance to the change, they quickly adapted. Sheri, who was sixteen, got a job as a maid at the Lake Hotel cabins. At the age of fourteen, Scott was too young for such jobs, but he quickly found his niche, cleaning and waxing cars for employees. In Atlantic City —where the residents were frugal, and their pickup trucks were coated with dust or mud—he certainly could not have earned money doing that.

Scott came to Atlantic City one weekend to help me pack the old Chevy truck with my few belongings and the rest of Terry's. As I vacuumed the rug in my 100-year-old log cabin, tears slid down my cheeks, remembering my months as a single woman before Terry and I got together. A woman friend questioned my decision to follow my man to Yellowstone and turn my back on my independent life at Atlantic City, where I had hauled my own water and bucked my own firewood. "It's not like he asked me to move to New York City!" I told her. "I want to experience living in Yellowstone." My words helped convince myself as much as her. I was saying goodbye to one life and moving into another, and change had never been easy for me. Giving up my cabin meant that I was committing myself to Terry and our future together. There is always risk involved in such decisions, but I felt ready this time.

Among the residents at Lake, the favored game of chance each summer was guessing when the ice would finally clear from Yellowstone Lake. Since the process can take weeks, the gamblers agreed to use the day when we could see clear water from Bridge Bay Marina to Stevenson Island, a distance of about two miles. I took a geology class in June, and the geologist took us to the lake outlet so we could watch plates of ice glide toward Fishing Bridge. He was using them to illustrate a tectonics theory, but our class was too busy watching a muskrat on an ice floe, munching on some delicacy stuck in the ice. We hoped he would disembark before the 100-foot drop at Upper Falls. The geologist's fascinating tales of lava rivers and giant glaciers failed to hold our attention when we could watch live harbingers of spring such as the muskrat and the loon, which seemed to stand on one wing as he did his mating dance with no potential mate in sight. How loony. We loony humans always felt strangely relieved when spring once again arrived. Like being surprised at a sunrise.

As the snow melted and icy torrents gushed toward the lake, Terry's road crew kept busy preventing washouts. Traveling tourist kids watched longingly as these big boys used giant toys to scoop ditches and sculpt dikes along the road. The snowmelt gradually raised the level of the 7,700-foot high lake. Lester Warwood was considered the expert on lake levels. A big, slow-talking Montana rancher, he had been known to carry a newborn bloody calf in his new Lincoln Continental before he semi-retired from ranching and came to work for Yellowstone in the early 1970s. When we met Lester, he had been measuring water levels at the marina for fourteen years, and he said it usually peaked the first week in July. In 1974, the water rose seven feet with the melt. Imagine. By my calculations, that meant an increase of five percent (or so) in volume for the giant, 132-square-mile lake, despite all the gallons pouring through the outlet into the Yellowstone River. I figured it took 198 billion gallons of melted snow floating on top of the lake to raise it seven feet. I bet the North Dakota farmers noticed when Yellowstone water swelled the Missouri River there.

We barely saw our winter neighbors during the hectic summer season. They were caught up in the flurry of "Yellowstone City." Ranger Alice Siebecker and her colleagues were called out at all hours for traffic accidents, collisions between cars and animals, and fire alarms at the dormitories. We learned a lot about modern park ranger work by eavesdropping on the park radio. One night campers exchanged gunfire in a dispute over firewood. Assembled guns were illegal in the park at the time. When Alice and the other rangers arrived at the crime scene, there were six suspects, three of whom had guns, including a gun that had been reported stolen. One suspect was a druggie who had abducted his two children. The campground had turned into an urban crime scene. The next day, Alice was back to dealing with bear jams and having to dispatch an injured porcupine that had been hit by a car. In her dual role as our unofficial social worker, Alice also kept busy counseling distraught wives, lecturing drunks, and advising young employees.

We caught sight of Lorie on the garbage crew sometimes. Collecting trash was important year round in Yellowstone, since grizzly bears tended to invade campgrounds in search of edibles. Modern Yellowstone garbage cans were specially designed to thwart hungry bears from opening them, unlike earlier eras when the Park Service had used easily accessible cans. Now the philosophy was to force the bears back into the woods to earn an honest living. The garbage crew called themselves "Bear Forage Technicians" instead of garbage collectors. We summer residents learned we could not leave food in our cars because a bear might break in; we could not have gardens; and no bird feeders or barbecue grills could be left outside.

When Lorie started her summer job, she had to lift 200 garbage cans daily, each weighing up to forty-five pounds. A couple of the guys privately predicted the new girl would keel over and die; she was that out of shape. Instead Lorie turned garbage collection into a game: The Trash Man Can-Can. Two workers would jump off the back of the garbage truck and race each other to the can. After lifting the heavy, bear-proof lid, each person would lift the bag full of trash and sling it into the hopper with the right arm while simultaneously stuffing a new bag into the can with the left. As an added sound effect, Lorie gave the cans a quick kick, which also assured that the lids dropped tightly. A good driver would start rolling just as the lids banged back into place. Their dance left the campers cheering and laughing.

We spent much of the summer getting to know our neighbor Yellowstone Lake, which was also much different in the summer than the winter. The sky and the lake reflected colors and moods, the interface sometimes indistinguishable. When the sky angered, it enraged the sea too, releasing monsters from the depths that consumed far more victims than grizzly bears ever had. More than 100 people had drowned in Yellowstone by 1993—when Lee H. Whittlesey completed his book, *Death in Yellowstone: Accidents and Foolhardiness in the First National Park*—more than from any other causes he investigated.

The sea monsters nearly devoured us one day. We had bought a houseboat and spent nearly every weekend exploring the lake. Dad, Sue, and Scott had joined us for a three-day weekend in the lake's South Arm. The day had drifted by in the tranquil bays, with us casting, catching cutthroat trout, and chatting. The bronze-colored, red-cheeked cutthroat flashed in the water as they dove and fought. Sue caught the first of several fish. Hers was eighteen inches long, and its majesty made me glad for the regulations that required putting the big ones back.

Just as we were savoring the last mouthfuls of a trout dinner inside the boat cabin, Scott noticed dark clouds to the southwest. To avoid the approaching lightning storm, Terry started the houseboat across the channel that connects the lake to West Thumb. To get home, we had to cut ourselves loose from the security of the shoreline, exposing ourselves to the full force of waves that build in the thumb. Scott, the teenager on board, watched the approaching clouds with glee, craving a violent storm.

As the waves grew to three feet high, Terry steered to quarter into the waves. Then the engine quit, and the boat turned broadside toward the wind. The canoe on the top deck flew off the rail and hung by its rope, banging down the port side, barely audible above the roaring wind. Six-foot waves crashed over the deck. As Terry frantically tried to restart the motor, a glass coffee pot flew out of the cupboard and shattered on the floor. Flashlights, ropes, and dishes hurtled through the air; Scott scrambled for life jackets for everyone; my father lunged for the sea anchor and forced his way through the kitchen rubble to the back deck. Outside the picture windows, we could see only water, wet nothingness where a skyline—and a coastline—should have been.

After what seemed like hours, the engine started, and Terry steered us out of the channel and beached the boat at Sand Point. Scott leaped out and kissed the ground. We all began chattering at once, wired on adrenalin. As we laughed off our terror, my body chemicals slowed. I made Scott promise not to wish another storm upon us. Dad and Sue told us that A&W Adventures were acquiring a bad name. We later determined that a partially clogged fuel line had made the engine quit. Through Terry's boatsmanship and good fortune, we escaped, but I never saw the lake as benign again. The cutthroat must have convinced the sea monsters to demonstrate how it feels to be caught by the throat and then released.

When fall arrived, Lorie emceed the annual Maintenance Awards Ceremony that she and her friend Rossa had created. Despite being a woman in an overwhelmingly man's world, Lorie established a casual camaraderie with her fellow workers, cemented with her self-deprecating sense of humor. She said she couldn't shirk her responsibilities by batting her eyelashes; she never felt cute enough to get away with it. At the fall Maintenance Awards

Ceremony, she presented innovative, sometimes profane objects d'art such as

- the Light Bulb Award (a hard hat with a light bulb on the top for the person with the best idea),
- Golden Plunger (a yellow-painted toilet plunger for the best worker on the cleaning crew),
- Macho Man (a date with the anatomically correct, inflatable doll named Ruby Red Lips who had been rescued from the garbage),
- Sweet Personality Award (person most likely to annoy people) and
- Square Patch Award (a hunk of asphalt for the person who made the best road patches).

Gradually the students and teachers who worked summers in the park returned to their schools and the facilities closed, one by one. We missed the post office and the gas station, but we did not miss the hordes of summer. The road gates were locked, and Yellowstone became our private park again.

When I went out to Bridge Bay Campground for my daily run, I listened to Beryl Markham's tales of crossing East Africa by horseback. She said, "When you must leave a place, leave it quickly and do not look back. The future is in a cloud, but as you enter the cloud, it becomes clearer." I was sure that was a message I would need to remember one day, but for that moment, I was too distracted. I was remembering our niece Michelle telling us she hesitated to wear earphones while she ran in Portland, Oregon. "Too dangerous." I suppose she meant muggers and rapists, but I had to keep my ears open for bison snorts. Or bears. People who spent much time in areas frequented by grizzly bears told us we would know if a bear was near. Just open your senses, and if the hairs on the back of your neck tingle, pay attention. I wished that my senses were as acute as my dog's. We couldn't figure out why he was quivering one evening when we visited someone's apartment. The next day, we learned there was a grizzly under the porch.

With no people, the critters didn't take long to reoccupy their turf. The little trees planted in the Bridge Bay Campground meadow seem to be faring okay so far. It looked like some strange vegetable zoo, with the trees on the inside of six-foot cages and the animals looking in. Alice warned the tree planting crew that they would need fences, but at first they scoffed. "We should let nature take care of itself." Then they saw the remnants after a feisty bison bull took advantage of one of the little trees, horning it again and again just to watch it bleed.

After a noisy thunderstorm crashed through the darkness one night, I drove out to Gull Point Drive for my morning run. Watching steam rise from the lake's surface, you would have thought that dawn ended an ice age. During the last few million years, glaciers born on the lake had oozed southward toward Jackson's Hole. The geologists said that if the temperature dropped only a few degrees, it could happen again. The average temperature in the park was only thirty-three degrees Fahrenheit. Amongst the forest shadows on shore, I heard only the thud of my feet and the ravens, screeching like primeval beasts. Then upon the command of a bigger, deeper-voiced leader, they rose and swished a black curtain across the lake. When it lifted, the season's last pelican glided whitely through the mist on a sheet of obsidian.

In the quieter fall days, we started thinking again about a wedding. Scott and Sheri had returned to school in California. Terry and I were a little nervous about getting hitched even though we had been going together for four years. I was part of a generation that distrusted old institutions, as evidenced by the fact that I was thirty-six and had never married. Terry had seen too many other people's relationships fall apart after marriage, when assaulted by differing expectations. However, our friends in Atlantic City promised to make a quilt for us if we got married. We had seen the quilts, and we wanted one. Our friend Philippina Halstead painted the area's historic buildings and flowers on them, and most of the fifty community members signed them with liquid embroidery.

We recently had attended a wedding where, after the ceremony, we saw the bride sobbing and dragging her train through the mud, looking for her husband. I felt she was stressed out by the details of planning a big, complicated event for many people. I wanted something simple. On October 5, 1985, we drove to Cody to meet the justice of the peace, Dad and Sue, and our three witnesses, Bruce and Mary McCormack and Mary's daughter, Molly. I wore a dress borrowed from a friend.

Terry rushed off as soon as we hit town, and I smiled, assuming he was going to buy me flowers. No, when he came back, he proudly showed me the new lunch box he had found for himself. Meanwhile, Mary handed me a bouquet purchased by my distant friend, Lorna. Hmmm. A reminder: Don't rely upon the man for everything just because you are now married. Remember your friends and how important they are to you. The husband can't and won't fulfill all your needs.

We shared our simple vows at the feet of Sacajawea's statue in the Buffalo Bill Historical Museum courtyard while Mary played a tape of our favorite guitar player, Phil Heywood, on her boom box. Afterwards, Dad and Sue bought us all dinner at the historic Irma Hotel (built in 1902 for Buffalo Bill). Terry and I drove back to our home in the quadraplex at Lake. Our Yellowstone friends gave a chivaree, banging on pots and pans to celebrate the occasion. A few months later, our friends at Atlantic City held a reception for us, preceded by a hilarious mock wedding, and gave us the promised quilt. The sign announcing the celebration said, "Another A&W Adventure."

CHAPTER SIX

Coming of Age in Yellowstone

They strove to be equal to the demands of the day and asked no special help or treatment.... Women had no special stake in asserting their bravery or their prowess.

—LILLIAN SCHLISSEL

WOMEN'S DIARIES OF THE WESTWARD JOURNEY

O UR NEXT-DOOR NEIGHBOR, LORIE, KNEW SNOW INTIMATELY. She spent her first winter in Yellowstone two years before we arrived. At the age of twenty most young women would have been hanging out with friends of the same age, experimenting with ideas and independence and dating. Instead, Lorie was surrounded by snow and adult couples several decades older than her. The Lilleys and the Rollers watched out for Lorie just as they would have their own daughter, inviting her to dinner, fretting about her safety, and freely expressing their judgments about her social life. Chris Lilley and Alice Roller recognized her need for female companionship, and Hume Lilley helped her advance her career.

I called Chris one cold January night to see if I should worry about Lorie, who hadn't arrived home from her trip to Bozeman,

Montana. Living next door, I could usually hear when she came in. Normally I wouldn't have worried. Lorie had been snowmobiling for years, and when she went out to visit friends, she frequently stretched her weekends to the limit, waiting until after dark to snowmobile back to her solitary life at Lake. But it was below zero and she had 6,000 miles on her machine. Night trips into the park relied upon faith—faith in one's machine, faith that the roads hadn't drifted shut, and faith that no bison or moose had decided to take possession of the road. It was hard to retain such faith, especially with older machines. By the time that any of us had lived in the park for long, we had all been stranded at least once.

Even daytime encounters with bison could be daunting; some of the bulls weighed 2,000 pounds. One day, a big, bull bison blocked the road. When Lorie and her fellow roof shoveler approached him on snowmobiles, he suddenly turned and charged. Gary jumped off his machine and started running toward the trees. Watching the bucking, kicking animal spin toward her, Lorie turned her machine around and drove off the road, dodging the trees at full throttle. Lorie and Gary frantically looked for a tree to climb. Suddenly the bison stopped and vented his rage upon the trees, tearing out several small lodgepole pines by the roots.

Nighttime encounters were even more hair-raising. Terry and I tried to avoid traveling after dark whenever we could partly because others avoided traveling at night, which limited rescue possibilities. One frigid night during Terry's first winter, we listened in horror to radio traffic from an employee who had been hit by another snowmobiler on his way home from closing the bar at Old Faithful. Knocked unconscious and with a shattered leg, he had to wait for rescuers to transform a tracked vehicle into an ambulance and lumber to his side. By the time they arrived, he had nearly frozen.

Lorie figured if she got into trouble, she could count on her radio. However, sometimes the batteries went dead, or you broke down in a dead spot where radio waves couldn't reach anyone. Lorie's radio rescued her once before when Gertrude (her snowmobile) betrayed her late one evening. The road was hard packed with no new snow to lubricate the snowmachine's slide rails, so they heated up and melted the rubber track, stopping her machine dead in its own tracks at Norris, twenty-five miles from her car and twenty-five miles from home. Lorie was usually too hard-headed to call for help, but there was no other traffic so she called her boss, Hume. Terry went along with Hume to haul back her machine. When they arrived, she hurriedly repacked her groceries on the sled in the dark. One of the elastic bungee cords popped loose, the metal hook raking her cheek. When they finally got home at 11 P.M., they realized her face was covered with blood. Lorie promised to make a safety movie on how not to stand when you stretch bungee cords.

As the days grew longer, Lorie had time to ski with me after work some days, and I heard more of her stories. She called it "happy hour" when we strapped on our skis and took off together. As a winterkeeper, she shoveled snow off the Lake area government buildings' roofs—but Lorie quickly discovered she was afraid of heights. At first, working on the steep roofs would leave her trembling with fear. Her boss at the time never knew. "I was glad to get a job for what I was willing to do, not for my looks." As with many women on the frontier, she appreciated the economic opportunity. To claim her stake, she had to prove up. The work would have challenged anyone. Depending upon the temperatures, the snow could be six to ten feet deep and heavy.

Snow loads of 150 pounds per square foot of roof surface occur during heavy winters, according to veteran winterkeeper Jeff Henry in his book, *Snowshoes, Coaches, and Cross Country Skis: A Brief History of Yellowstone Winters*. That translates to a total of

4,800 pounds supported by just one sheet of plywood on the roof decking, he stated. With temperatures that don't rise above freezing for months at a time, snow loads just get heavier and heavier. Wind creates cornices that overhang the roof edges, further stressing the roof and the winterkeepers.

For the flat roofs, her first boss provided a huge shovel, big enough to scoop up a snowmobile. Full of wet snow, it weighed a good hundred pounds. Even her six-foot, four-inch male partner could not push it alone. The two of them would "run" behind the shovel, trying to shove the snow off the edge without flying off themselves. Her first boss initially criticized her for not working as fast as her male partner, but her partner knew how hard she worked, and he defended her.

Park Service roof shovelers sometimes wore crampons strapped to their boots—metal teeth similar to those worn by mountain climbers—that helped considerably on the wooden shingled roofs. But they were little help on metal roofs. Some roofs were easy. To reduce the snow load over the quadraplex where we lived, Lorie just clambered over the drifts at the back of the building—no need for a ladder. One winter all of us skied onto the roof of the hospital and skied off, just to say that we had.

Often Lorie shoveled roofs alone all day. When the snow was deep enough on the roofs, she reached up with a long saw to cut refrigerator-sized blocks. Then she used the shovel to loosen the blocks from the side—not from below—and send them crashing to the ground. The roof shovelers learn that if a roof started sliding with them, throw the shovel to the side so they would not land on top of it and potentially break bones.

In her solitude, Lorie tended to brood, and by the time she jumped off a completed roof, she would be "spitting ice cubes." As an antidote, she turned to rock and roll music, especially on steep roofs. When a particularly steep roof threatened to unnerve her, she sang "Roof Top Surfin'" to the tune of the old Beach

All winter the park's winterkeepers must remove snow to keep roofs from caving in. Jeff Henry, a Yellowstone winterkeeper and a professional photographer, provided this picture of himself on the Hamilton Store dormitory at Old Faithful in 1997, a year when the snow on the ground was twenty-two feet deep. (© Jeff Henry/Roche Jaune Pictures, Inc.)

Boys song. Country music worked better for the flat roofs because pushing the big shovels felt a lot like doing the country swing. Sometimes she listened to books on tape as she shoveled.

That first winter in 1982, Lorie had arrived for the job wearing a splint on her arm as the result of a car accident in the park three months earlier. More than a hundred pounds overweight, she could barely squeeze into her size eighteen uniform. Although she grew up in Montana, she had only been on a snowmobile three times before she bought Gertrude. On her first weekend off, Lorie headed out from Lake with Gertrude at full throttle. "I was dressed like Nanuk of the North." Lacking both mobility and snowmobile technique, she hit a bump in the intersection at Fishing Bridge and flew off, rolling like a barrel down the road. She picked herself up, dusted off, and looked hurriedly around to be sure no one saw her. Since it happened just a mile from Lake, she contemplated turning around and returning to her safe, warm apartment. Instead, she climbed back on. She had to snowmobile if she wanted to keep her job.

The days were short and the nights long. Loneliness nearly overwhelmed her. She spent hours in the tub, reading. Her first Christmas Eve away from home, the power went out, leaving her huddled alone in the dark by her wood stove. Everyone who had park radios was entertained that night, listening to the communication center staff sing Christmas carols to a Montana Power Company crew, stuck in the snow, as the crew tried to find the cause of the power outage. However, she lacked even that solace since she had no park radio at the time. So she wrestled with her memories until finally she went to bed. She took control in the coming years and always invited our family for pizza on Christmas Eve, no matter how many guests we might have.

The work became easier as she got stronger and learned to wax the shovel and avoid standing stiff-legged. Standing that way took more energy. She discovered the fun of jumping off after completing a roof. When Hume took over as the Lake foreman, he fashioned a shovel with a short handle more appropriate for her height. She learned to like Christmas at Lake and the small town feeling, not having to lock doors. She came to value her time alone, took up cross-stitch and knitting, and found a television and VCR. She got a cat, Minkie, so she would have someone to talk to about her day.

Nothing seemed to scare Lorie, as far as I could tell, but we both were spooked one day when we came upon a bison carcass during our evening ski. The little hairs on the back of my neck rose with primitive instinct: We knew in our guts that we were low in the hierarchy of predators interested in this prize. As we hurriedly skied away, we heard coyotes howling on the ridge top. Another day, she took me as a passenger around the lakeshore to Mary Bay where we encountered a long stretch of dry pavement. Snowmobiles can't be steered without snow, we both knew, and we were sliding sideways toward a big bull bison. When she finally got her machine stopped, we were fifteen feet in front of his nose. He just looked at us like, "Please don't make me have to get up, dummies."

The snow fell heavy and deep in Yellowstone. Our golden retriever Sarge could stand on the snow and look down at us and Lorie through the front windows of our ground floor apartments. One day we were trapped inside when a load of snow slid off the roof. We had to shove the storm door open a few inches and dig ourselves out using a spatula as a trowel. Then Terry removed the storm door, and I sculpted three nice, broad steps with manageable risers and comfortable treads to replace the otter-slide entrance down to our apartment. The next day, another load slid off the roof burying my steps and blocking Lorie's storm door. Lorie should have been an expert at predicting when roofs would slide, but not this time. She telephoned us saying she was trapped inside. The snow blocked our front windows nearly completely.

Chris said a flying saucer could have landed right outside, and we never would have known it.

Along with shoveling roofs, Lorie was responsible for dumping the community's trash. During the summer, maintenance workers compacted the trash and hauled it in garbage trucks 103 miles to Livingston, Montana. During the winter, however, the trash was collected and stored at the transfer station. The first time she pulled off the main road and into the untracked powder with the heavy sled of garbage, her machine immediately sank. Lacking a radio, she set out on foot for the shop, two miles away. A passing stranger taught her how to utilize her body weight as leverage to pry a heavy machine out of the muck, tricks that she later taught me: Unhook the sled from the machine; pack the snow around the machine by either stomping with the feet or lying down and rolling in it; hold the throttle and run alongside the machine until it gets to firmer ground.

Listening to Lorie's stories later, it was hard to imagine her as a novice at wintering in Yellowstone. By the time we met her, Lorie had lost the extra hundred pounds through a combination of aerobic exercise routines and hard work. I marveled at her skills and independence. She could pack a snowmobile sled full of cargo, ride drifted roads, and dig out a stuck machine as well as almost anyone in the park, better than most. Watching her gave me hope that one day I, too, would be able to travel solo safely and not be such a sissy.

One time Hume sent Lorie to Mammoth to pick up snowmachine oil for the government machines. The foreman there added up the weight of the cargo: 240 pounds. Did she think her machine could manage? Lorie would have to maneuver the loaded sled through the bumpy, little winding trail from the maintenance area to the groomed road and bounce it for fifty miles. Her counterpart from Grant had failed. He had packed the cases of oil on their sides, and several cans in each case had broken. When

Lorie delivered her cargo back to Lake without any breakage, she radioed Hume in triumph. "A piece of cake," she told him. I shared Lorie's pride in such accomplishments. Unlike the rest of us whose lives were centered outside of the park, Lorie's adult life started in Yellowstone. Yellowstone was her classroom for learning about working in a man's world, a pioneer in her field. Some of her instructors hoped that she would flunk. Because of Lorie's humor and bravado, we didn't detect until years later what a toll the life had taken on her.

The garbage detail presented its own challenges. Even in the frigid temperatures, the transfer station's aromas attracted animals. Peering out from under a pine bough, a pine marten looks like an under-sized brown bear with a tan chest, about the size of a house cat. Members of the weasel family, they weigh only about two pounds. They didn't look cute to the squirrels—their prey—or to Lorie when they leaped snarling and hissing into her face from the garbage. To cope with the marauders, Lorie learned to take the offensive. Flinging open the door of the transfer station, she shouted, "Honey, I'm home," to scare them into hiding.

One snowy November morning, she pulled up to the transfer station with a sled full of smelly garbage. She started to shout her usual greeting, but immediately she noticed something was wrong. Big boxes—too big for the martens to move—had been strewn around. The door jam was ripped up and had bloody teeth marks in it. Backing out quickly, she raced to her snowmachine, pulled frantically on the rope to start her reluctant snowmobile and raced back to the shop. She was convinced a grizzly bear was in the transfer station. The guys scolded her saying, "November 20 is too late for a bear; they are all hibernating by now." Lorie was right, however. Bear Number 83 had forced open the big, heavy door and slipped inside, apparently intent upon spending the winter there, but her cub was still outside. The mother bear was old, cantankerous, and mean. After the rangers trapped the bear, Lorie felt vindicated. "I would rather be a coward than an eaten-up brave person," she said.

For her social life Lorie primarily depended upon weekends outside the park. Coming home late was not unusual for her. On that cold January night, I told myself she was snow wise and that her radio had rescued her before. But then Lorie called and said her cargo sled had been stolen! Arriving at the parking lot at dusk with her groceries, she found only her snowmachine and its empty hitch. She had no way to carry her purchases into the park, and she had paid $150 for the sled. That news upset all of us who left our cars unguarded near the park entrances for months at a time. When we went out to get groceries, we left the snowmobiles and cargo sleds there while we drove our cars to town for two or three days. Often we left the snowmobile keys in the ignition. No one needs a key to steal one. Just unplug the ignition switch, pull the rope, and take off.

Fortunately, a friend spotted Lorie's distinctively painted sled parked at Old Faithful. The next day Hume left for Old Faithful well before dawn, picked up the stolen sled, and delivered it to Lorie at Mammoth, snowmobiling more than 200 miles. That night Lorie dreamed she found the thief and beat him to the ground with her snowmobile helmet. The man had violated her trust, but her friends in the community had stood by her. Terry suggested that Lorie paint flowers on her recovered sled to discourage any "real man" from being seen with it.

CHAPTER SEVEN

Zero Visibility

The best moments of our lives come when a person's body or mind is stretched to its limits in the thrill of trying to accomplish something difficult and worthwhile.

—MIHALY CSIKSZENTMIHALYI

FLOW: THE PSYCHOLOGY OF OPTIMAL EXPERIENCE

*I*N THE INTERMOUNTAIN WEST, THE WINTER OF 1986 WAS TO be remembered for the Presidents' Day Storm. Terry and I certainly remembered that storm, and I had written evidence—an addendum to my Last Will and Testament that I scrawled on top of Sylvan Pass.

Midway through my second winter of snowmobiling, I finally ventured out by myself without Terry. I had been adjusting to the isolation and the subzero temperatures rather well until some phone calls in December. My stepmother Susie's father died, and I was not there to grieve with them. My brother Steve lived in Colorado and was recovering from a serious accident, but I had not seen him in many months. My sister Becky and her family lived in the South Pacific, and with our mail delays added to the normal four-week turnaround time for airmail, I felt estranged from their lives. Because of Terry's work schedule and my reluctance to go out without him, I had missed a birthday ski trip and several other events that I normally would have attended. I was spoiled compared with most people in the world and considered such mobility a basic freedom. The dependence upon other people and Mother Nature frustrated me, and I realized it could breed resentment. So when one of my editors asked me to attend the annual Council of Energy Resource Tribes meeting in Denver, I agreed.

Little did we know that a historic storm was on its way toward Yellowstone. My exit trip the week before was excitement enough for me to last all winter. My first twenty-two miles from Lake around the lakeshore and up to the pass was uneventful, but I encountered a short snow squall on top of Sylvan, and the light turned flat. Not being able to see whether I was going uphill or down, I slammed my machine into a pile of snow left by a recent snowslide, getting it thoroughly stuck. I struggled to get it to move but soon realized I did not have the strength. By then it was really dark; there was no one else on the road, and I had no radio to call for help. Employee spouses were not allowed to carry government radios. So I started walking the eight miles to the East Entrance Ranger Station.

Like a city dweller figuring out which neighborhoods were safe to walk in at night, I knew by then what to fear and what not to fear. No bison ever crossed over the pass so I didn't have to worry about them on the east side. Since it was February, I knew the bears would all be hibernating. Moose would have been the worst to encounter in the dark, but Terry had told me he never saw any moose on the east side. I could not get lost because of the huge piles of snow that Terry had sculpted into berms on both sides of the road. My eight-mile stroll gave me plenty of time to think about Lorie and her many solo expeditions across the pass to collect water samples from the East Entrance housing area.

What would she have done to extract her snowmobile if this had happened to her?

When Terry did not hear from me at the expected time, he rode up to look for me, despite suffering from a fever and bad cough. When he arrived at the ranger station ten minutes after I did, he said my tracks looked as if I actually traveled sixteen miles instead of eight. Without a flashlight or moonlight, I wandered back and forth across the road until I bumped into the snow mounds along the shoulders and corrected my direction. Because of mild temperatures, I actually enjoyed my stroll, but I was not happy that Terry had to ride thirty miles out and thirty miles back in as a result of the escapade. My Aunt Jane reinforced my identity as an adventurer when I called to tell her about walking off Sylvan Pass in the dark. After a long silence, she said, "You're just like your mother was. You like that sort of thing, don't you?" I could not have been prouder.

In Denver, I collected thick environmental impact statements and tribal codes at the meeting as voraciously as ever, despite knowing I would have to cart them across Sylvan Pass. I was working on a book on American Indian energy development as well as the article I had been assigned, and I planned to pore over the papers at home. Driving back from Denver, I stopped to visit friends in Lander and shared my anxiety about my return trip into the park. One of my friends, Berthenia, who had traveled alone throughout Asia as a young woman, couldn't understand. Faced with her unflappable composure, I felt foolish.

As it turned out, my fretting was more than justified. Soon after I had left the park and Terry had returned to Lake, a massive blizzard hit Yellowstone and raged for five days. The interior villages were cut off from all directions. High winds created huge drifts across Swan Lake Flats to the north and through Hayden Valley (between Canyon and Lake). To the south, the winds created fourteen-foot finger drifts along the lakeshore, two or three feet apart, with bare pavement in-between. With the high winds, the groomers in the districts couldn't keep the roads open. No one could get out, and no one could get in. Alice Siebecker's fiancé, Brian Crandell, called her from Bozeman, Montana, to say the storm had changed his plans. "That's what I love about the West," Brian said. "There's no question of control. It's humbling."

Not everyone felt that way. Employees couldn't travel to other districts to fix furnaces or pick up parts, much less get out of the park to buy groceries or visit their wives and children. Lake was totally cut off from the rest of the park. Helicopters could not have reached anyone who had a medical emergency.

East Gate Ranger Bob Mahn reported that tons of snow had accumulated above the avalanche chutes on Sylvan. The maintenance crew knew they could trust Bob's judgment about conditions on the pass; he always gave slow and detailed descriptions of his road. A maverick who cared more about people than rules, he was appreciated more by maintenance workers and visitors than by some fellow rangers. If Bob said the snowload was bad, it was bad. Snow had to be blasted loose before anyone dared to cross. Finally the storm seemed to subside, and Terry was able to clear the north-south road. This allowed the avalanche crew (a gunner and a loader) to travel from Mammoth and follow Terry's grooming machine as it crawled slowly eastward toward the pass. When they reached the avalanche gun platform, several hours later, the gunnery crew loaded the seventy-five millimeter recoilless rifle and aimed for the targets half a mile away above the avalanche chute. Boom! Snow thundered down the mountain and over the road, creating wind that roared like a freight train and blasted them at their platform half way up the other side. Boom! Boom! Another huge avalanche and another. Finally after ten shots, when they could see no more large cornices over the chutes on the opposite mountain, they quit and headed home.

But Terry's job had just begun. The avalanches had obliterated the road with a pile of snow and debris thirty feet deep and one hundred yards long. Over the two winters he had groomed Sylvan dozens of times, and he knew the Sylvan Pass terrain like the face of his best friend—or worst enemy. But after the storm, snow mixed with broken trees covered all the landmarks as well as the snow stakes and guardrails along the roadway.

I was waiting at the East Entrance for a ride home, but I wasn't Terry's only motivation for getting across. He loved challenges, and the Presidents' Day Storm presented an opportunity to utilize his talent and his creativity. With little evidence of the old route over the pass, he could redesign the road. Unfortunately, his regular tool for sculpting—the DMC groomer—was in the shop for repairs so he was forced to use an old, worn out Piston Bully groomer with no hydraulic pressure to keep down the groomer's front blade. Thus he couldn't carve the dense tons of cement-like snow to eliminate the steep side slope. His groomer crawled crab-like across the pass, its nose turned forty-five degrees uphill to keep from sliding toward the canyon below. If he had gotten in trouble, he was on his own. No one could have reached him by snowmobile under those conditions. Finally, at 7 P.M., after twelve hours in the groomer, he reached the East Gate, and we reunited.

Early the next morning, Terry and I left the East Entrance in the groomer and headed up the road, plowing through drifts that had accumulated during the night. Three hours later, we reached the top and encountered...nothing. Where we should have seen trees, the hundred-foot drop-off, and granite cliffs on the uphill side, we saw nothing—only howling whiteness. Obviously we could proceed no farther. Sylvan could be harrowing even when you could see the trail. Since Terry normally operated the groomer only two to three feet from the drop-off, he needed to know where that drop-off was.

Terry called the Yellowstone Communication Center with his

report, and they announced over the radio, "Be advised. Sylvan Pass is experiencing zero visibility." I pacified myself with philosophical questions. If we weren't up there in the blizzard to not see it, would it still be zero visibility? Is that the same as being invisible? Can a pass "experience" anything? The pass's name derived from Latin: *Silvanus* is the god of the woods. Our neighbor, Lorie, always thought of Sylvan Pass as animate, referring to it reverently as "The Lady." She didn't want to show any sign of disrespect for fear of Sylvan's reprisal.

Although my rational mind laughed at that, I found myself watching for manifestations of The Lady's mood and our fate. During our slow, methodical travels up and down the pass, we listened to music cassettes on the tape deck he had bought for the groomer. Gordon Lightfoot sang, "When I woke up this morning, something inside of me told me this was going to be my day." My day for what? I tried to stop thinking of the snow slide that slammed into my family and me twenty years earlier when we were skiing off Berthoud Pass. We were trapped in heavy, wet cement until my father dug us out, and my sister, Becky, was lucky to be alive. She was buried two feet below the surface until our father found her half an hour later. None of us ever forgot that lesson about the power of snow.

After staring at nothingness for two hours, Terry and I turned back to report our defeat to Ranger Bob. He understood the wisdom of turning back in such a storm, especially after an experience he'd had in Hayden Valley. Snowmobiling homeward late one night, he didn't see Montana Power Company's big Tucker Sno-cat until his snowmachine was already between its revolving tracks, the red warning triangle in his face. By then it was too late. The Sno-cat's metal bed put a good dent in his helmet, but the Montana Power crew never knew he had hit them. Bob never told them. Since Bob didn't drink, we trusted that it had been a ferocious storm, much like this one.

When we went down to eat at Pahaska Tepee, the restaurant was almost empty. We saw the owner, Bob Coe, who was exasperated and a little embarrassed about the storm. In addition to providing food and lodging for winter visitors, Pahaska rented out skis and snowmobiles. Perhaps he had himself to blame for the storm; he said he had prayed for snow for the past two months. Presidents' Day was usually one of the three biggest weeks for his snowmobile trade. He shook his head incredulously as he put up the sign saying, "Sylvan Pass closed indefinitely. 109 inches in the last ten days." He couldn't even get his snowmobiles back from the west side of the park. When a group of snowmobilers couldn't get back through the park, they rented a car at West Yellowstone and drove 400 miles around the park to retrieve their vehicle from Pahaska, abandoning Pahaska's snowmobiles at West.

At Pahaska we ate dinner with Ranger Bob and his girlfriend, Grace Nutting. We were unaccustomed to seeing Bob—the perpetual bachelor—with someone by his side, but Terry and I had good instincts about people, and we could feel their affection for one another. We knew it would take an unusual woman to tie up with Bob, and Grace was certainly unusual. She was a pilot, had a master's in library science, and spoke six languages. She had grown up in New England, but Wyoming and its birds captured her heart so she cleaned campgrounds to make a living.

The second morning we started up the pass again. Hume Lilley, Terry's boss on the other side of the pass at Lake, was getting antsy, and who could blame him after a full week waiting out the storm? Without access to the park's hub, all plans were on hold. Hume called Terry on the radio, urging him to get the groomer back to Lake. Hume didn't like to back down to anybody, including Mother Nature when she got belligerent. He wanted to be in control. But Yellowstone demanded flexibility, changing plans to adapt to changing weather conditions. It wasn't an easy lesson for any of us. Terry didn't like being stuck when so much work awaited him on the other side. Even without Hume's call, Terry felt driven to reach Lake. He ached to tackle the pass again. His earlier trip across the pass had only momentarily satisfied his craving for challenge. But he knew better than to argue with Sylvan.

His temperament suited grooming. While my anxiety made me impatient to get up to the pass, he worked his way up the road through the new slides methodically. Terry liked to be prepared for anything and then not worry. His serene approach protected visitors—and his passenger—from accidents, but it drove Hume crazy, and sometimes I got frustrated by his being so meticulous and calm. It seemed I spent hours waiting for him to pack a snowmobile sled. On the groomer, Terry carried a sleeping bag, Sterno, matches, first aid kit, and food rations in case he got stuck or found an injured snowmobiler. Hume told him that was not necessary; Hume would come rescue him if the groomer got stuck. Terry appreciated Hume's fierce loyalty to our community and his willingness to fight the world on our behalf. But during Terry's first winter in the park, two rangers had called him to rescue them; the road was impassable to their snowmobiles. If the groomer got stuck on a day like that, what snowmobiler could get through to rescue him?

In his book *Deep Survival: Who Lives, Who Dies, and Why*, Laurence Gonzales talks about the people who die from inexperience, stupidity, or inattention when they are outdoors—skiing, snowmobiling, climbing, or hiking. "Most people operate in an environment of such low risk that action, inaction, or the vicissitudes of brains have few consequences....Mistakes spend themselves harmlessly and die out unnoticed instead of growing out of control."

In Yellowstone, mistakes matter. In his book *Death in Yellowstone*, historian Lee H. Whittlesey devoted an entire chapter to people who died in avalanches or from freezing. Terry thought ahead to avoid mistakes and got frustrated at seeing other people's foolish risks. One time Terry encountered a guy pulling a miniature log cabin on his sled behind his snowmobile. He had stopped on Sylvan in an avalanche path to eat lunch, blocking the groomer from passing. Terry, who normally would rather shoot himself than provide advice, told him, "That isn't very smart to park there." Another day Terry took the groomer out of the heated garage and started down the road. It was 60° below. The steering ran on hydraulics, and when the hydraulic fluid started cooling down and squealing, he got to thinking. "If I blow a hydraulic line, someone will have to come out and get me on a snowmobile." So he turned it around, went back, and put it in the garage. While people outside the park who craved adrenaline might read thrillers, watch horror movies, or have a love affair, our daily lives provided plenty of adrenaline.

The second day on Sylvan wasn't any better than the first so we turned tail again. When we reached the top on the third day, the winds still raged. Terry teased me, saying, "Just another A&W adventure." Finally the storm lifted long enough for us to start, across a landscape we hardly recognized. The first hurdle was a steep drift shaped like an elongated A-frame house, two stories tall. If I scaled it on foot, I could have easily straddled the peak. It was that narrow, but we weren't on foot. We were trying to get the old Piston Bully across, and its tracks were eleven feet wide. Terry's challenge was to climb the A-frame, cut off the top, and build a ramp to accommodate the tracks. As we started up, he used the plow blade to scrape off snow and push it toward the left, rolling back and forth to pack it, gaining only a couple of feet with each effort.

When we finally perched near the top, we heard a sound. "What's that banging?" I asked Terry, imagining an abominable snowman beating on the side of the cab, clearly too fantastic to endanger us. Instead, Terry said the track banged when it was suspended in the air, over the edge of the ramp he was building.

Not good. Why had I asked? If he had looked out his window, Terry could have peered through the track into the 300-foot-deep canyon. Instead, he was focusing on the job ahead. Not wanting to disturb his concentration, I wordlessly went through a mental checklist. Thinking of all the things that would fly around in the cab if we rolled down into the canyon, I put my helmet on. No seat belts—try to hold onto the seat. Put boots back on so I could at least crawl out of the wreckage. Get radio out so I could call for help. No roll bar—nothing I could do about that one. Except worry.

We'd probably get thrown out and lost in the resulting avalanche. Robert Frost's words swam through my head: "Some say the world will end in fire, some say in ice. From what I've tasted of desire, I hold with those who favor fire. But if I had to perish twice, I think I know enough of hate to say that for destruction ice is also great and would suffice." Pulling out my notebook, I began writing: "Jazmyn McDonald has my will, which wouldn't need to be changed except our joint account at Shoshone Bank in Cody should go to Sheri and Scott Wehrman. Our life insurance should also go to them. Signed, Marjane Ambler 2/22/86, Sylvan Pass."

Seeing my preparations out the corner of his eye, Terry didn't have time to feel offended, nor would he. He knew I trusted him. I was well aware that Terry was good with equipment. I had seen him compete in a motor grader rodeo where he cracked a raw egg with his blade, and I knew about his many safety awards. I would not have even gone up there on Sylvan in those conditions with anyone else, especially someone like Hume who might bludgeon his way forward, regardless.

Before those three days on the pass, I never had such a clear vision of what to worry about when Terry was working. He downplayed the danger, but there was a memorial on Red Mountain Pass in Colorado for three snowplow operators who died in separate incidents, so I was not easily reassured. A few weeks earlier the drum behind the DMC groomer filled up with warm, sticky snow and wouldn't turn. When he backed up, it slid over the edge. (In normal operation, the drum smoothes out the rough snow left by the groomer tracks.) By attaching chains at different places on the drum and the groomer and pulling, taking them off and reattaching again, he gradually got it back on the road. The operation took an hour and a half, right in the middle of an avalanche chute. When he finally walked through the door, I felt overjoyed, not knowing why he was two hours late.

I had asked Terry how he felt about going across those avalanche chutes so many times. He preferred the challenge of drifts and avalanche chutes to trundling along a relatively flat road at eight miles an hour, day after day, eight to ten hours a day. And he had a plan. If a slide came down and he could not outrun it, then he would turn his blade up into it and hope the groomer would stay on top. After planning, he pushed the worry out of his head. "If I don't deal with it that way, I might as well get another job." While another man might look braver as he barged ahead blindly, that man might be afraid to contemplate the danger, and thus more likely to get hurt.

An article in the Lakota Times quoted a woman whose husband was a Navy SEAL. "I depend upon him for certain things—taking the garbage out and plugging the car in," she said. Little, inconsequential parts of couple's routines, which suddenly—at separations—become substantial. I depend upon my husband for little things, too—starting the snowmachines, repairing them, taking the dogs out at night, repairing my glasses, washing the dishes. When he has a migraine, I do them myself and so avoid sliding into complete dependency. It's my defense against the Cinderella Complex. After his migraines, he always came back to me, and I relied on that.

Could I survive the loss of the things I really depended upon, the things the Lakota wife did not, perhaps could not, mention?

His cuddling against me all night, his gentle teasing, his devotion to me and our family. The man who spent most of a day sewing a bed for our dog. Who makes a religion out of packing the machines and the sled, but who did not say, "I told you so," when my improperly packed ski flew off my sled.

Once Terry succeeded in building his ramps and dismantling the snow A-frame, crossing the rest of the pass was merely tedious, not terrifying to me. As we started down the other side, Terry's shoulders and jaw loosened, and he grinned as he switched on the tape deck. The zero visibility experience had made some things clear to me. How could I have questioned trusting my bank account to this man when I entrusted my life to him so often? Descending toward the lake, we sang along with the bagpipes, not realizing that his lunch box had slid against the radio and keyed the microphone. Everyone in the park could hear us.

Down below Alice Siebecker was on the roof of the warming hut—miles from any homes or offices—when she suddenly heard strange music. She paused from her shoveling, puzzled by the foreign whine. A snowmobiler with a portable radio? No, Sylvan was still closed. Bagpipes? Could bagpipe music be coming out of the radio on her waist?

"Amazing Grace, how sweet the sound, that saved a wretch like me. I once was lost but now I'm found, was blind but now I see...."

CHAPTER 8
Yellowstone Has Teeth

Don't lose your fear. If you lose your fear, you lose your vigilance.
—RICK FEY, YELLOWSTONE LAKE BOAT RANGER

*B*EARS OCCUPY A DIFFERENT SPOT IN THE HUMAN PSYCHE than bison or other animals. When members of the Blackfeet tribe prepare for a bear hunt, they dress as if going to war and refer to the bear as "the man with the fur coat." Our friend and bear expert Jim Garry often said, "We humans think of ourselves at the top of the food chain. It's unnerving to discover we are not."

One day in November 1986, Ranger Alice Siebecker suggested I forgo my daily ski and stay inside. A sow grizzly was in the area, terrorizing the contractors remodeling Lake Hotel. When they walked from their dorm to their worksite each day, the bear charged. That day she had escalated the warfare, attacking the cook shack and trapping several workers huddled inside.

"We haven't done anything wrong. Why are we under house arrest?" I muttered to Sarge, our golden retriever. That fall I had purchased my first computer and was enjoying getting to know the new toy. After each day at the computer, however, I relied upon my evening ski to clear my brain, and the dog lived for his daily excursion. In truth, no one forced us to stay home. There was a reason why Alice and my other neighbors were especially nervous. Just a month earlier, rangers had noticed a car parked for several days at Otter Creek, near Canyon Village, fourteen miles from Lake. The situation seemed ominous: Binoculars, backpack, and camping gear had been left in full view as if the owner intended to return within minutes. When Alice made some calls, she discovered William J. Tesinsky had not shown up for work. His girlfriend was worried but had not known whom to call. She thought he was taking photographs in the Crazy Mountains of Montana.

Meanwhile, a grizzly was known to be roaming in the same general area south of Canyon. A bison carcass lay rotting across the Yellowstone River, but the bear was not feeding on the carcass as would have been expected. Why not? What was going on? Since this bear often roamed in populated areas, rangers had trapped her and equipped her with a radio collar that transmitted a signal all her own—Bear 59. Park rangers organized a search party near the abandoned car, and their equipment picked up Bear 59's signal. As they climbed a small hill near the abandoned car and shouldered their high-caliber rifles, no one spoke. They trudged side by side, struggling to keep their imaginations under control. When they crested the hill, they saw Bear 59—with a pair of human legs. They had to kill the grizzly to recover the body; they had no choice.

Even before the rangers returned from their gruesome duty, the phones were ringing with critics demanding to know why they had killed the bear. The grizzly bear symbolizes the wilderness to many people. If grizzlies are not safe in a 2.2-million-acre national park like Yellowstone, where can they live unmolested? One ranger's wife accosted her husband after he returned: The bear was only protecting her food. Why should that be a capital offense? For weeks, Tesinsky and the bear dominated conversations as we speculated about what happened. Everyone I talked with blamed the photographer, who apparently crept up and surprised the grizzly while she was eating yampa, a favorite plant in the bears' local cuisine. Judging from the setting on his camera lens and the position of his tripod, he was only twelve to fifteen feet from the bear. He left his long distance telephoto lens—a 1,000 millimeter—in the car. If he had used it instead, he and the bear might still be alive.

Over and over, we imagined the scenario. The grizzly probably made a bluff charge, as she had with other people in the Canyon area. Instead of backing off or playing dead, Tesinsky apparently held his ground, a sure sign of aggression to the bear. At what point did the bear start to see the man as protein rather than competition for her yampa patch? The weekend before the search, she twice had buried the man's partially consumed body after eating her fill. Did it begin to smell like food after the sun had warmed it for a while? If we had to choose a bear to cull from the gene pool, it might have been her. Bear 59 wasn't a good mom; she had abandoned at least two sets of cubs over the years. For his part, the photographer was known to push limits for the sake of a photo. Perhaps he hoped that a full-frame photo would be his ticket to fame.

Living and hiking in bear country, we all had been coached about what to do if we surprised a bear on the trail: Stand your ground, avert your eyes, and talk gently. However, if a bear charged and ran over you, play dead. Our neighbor, Barbara Pettinga, drilled this lesson into us. A ranger naturalist in the park for many years, she became well known when she survived an encounter with a grizzly. The bear charged her and she dropped to the ground, lying on her stomach and covering her neck with her hands. The bear turned her over twice, and apparently because he found no sign of aggression, he left Barbara battered but alive.

We appreciated grizzly bears. Earlier that summer when Jim Garry visited us, we all got up at 5 A.M. to go look for grizzlies and felt thrilled when we spotted one near Mary Bay, digging up yampa and searching for ground squirrels. We would rather watch them from the safety of our truck, however. We felt uneasy that fall of 1986 with so many bears in our neighborhood—at least four grizzlies, one with a cub, and two out at the East Entrance. Our neighbor Lorie told us she was tired of all the "dead body talk." It made her nervous. It was getting to me, too. Bears roamed my dreams each night. Seven bears chased me from room to room in a big house. When we reached the kitchen, they became very upset about a poster saying, "You can't outrun a grizzly, but you can outswim him." This idea sprang from the Lewis and Clark journals Terry and I had been reading.

Another night, my dreams swarmed with familiar dogs and wild beasts. Outside on the porch, a mountain lion stood on my foot, his claws drawing blood, while he hunted our dogs, Sarge and Banjo. That dream must have come from my worries about our pets and from Ranger Bob Mahn's stories the week before as we ate dinner outside the park at Absaroka Lodge, beneath a huge mountain lion pelt.

Bob and his wife, Grace Nutting, told us that despite Bear 104's constant presence in their housing area at the East Entrance and the restrictions placed on the employees there, they did not mind. Bear 104 had behaved herself. The tourists hadn't. One night a tourist reported being charged by a moose. An overly eager tourist had kicked the moose in the ribs because she was lying down, and he wanted her to stand up for a photograph. The next morning, while working in the campground, Grace glimpsed a moose calf wobbling after his mom, so new his ears still flopped. The mom must have been the same cow, kicked while in the early stages of labor. In our area, a man shot a bison with a slingshot while his son watched. Many tourists think they look docile and dumb, lying on the ground chewing their cuds like farm cows. You'd think the two-leggeds would notice the football player conformation—narrow hips and padded shoulders—and suspect that some aggressive genes might dwell within the huge bodies. One day we watched a bison in the corral area behind our apartment: He charged a park service horse and threw him into the air, spilling his guts all over the pasture. Bison instructed several human visitors each year about their territorial needs, inserting a horn and tossing the encroacher out of the way.

Thoughtless human behavior stressed the wildlife unnecessarily and also endangered the public. Telling the story about the moose, Grace shook her head and said, "Yellowstone has teeth. It will bite you when you turn your back." Anyone who lived in the park for long learned that lesson. She and Bob were both EMTs so they often dealt with death in their work. Rangers inevitably encounter tragedies. Some were normal for police officers anywhere: Administering emergency medical assistance, and when unsuccessful, breaking the news to the family.

Considering that millions of people visited Yellowstone each year, most of them encountering the full force of nature for the first time, deaths were surprisingly few. Over more than a century, only 300 people died from the park's more notorious threats—falling off cliffs, boiling in hot springs, and most rarely, being attacked by bears. In his 1995 book, *Death in Yellowstone: Accidents and Foolhardiness in the First National Park*, Lee H. Whittlesey reported that in the whole history of the park, only five people were killed by bears, while more than 100 drowned. Terry and I felt Yellowstone's teeth on our necks when a ferocious summer storm with six-foot waves threatened to roll our houseboat in Yellowstone Lake. Most of the visitors' deaths occurred in the summer and resulted from traffic accidents and heart attacks—taking weak hearts to high elevations and exerting them. At the time, twenty-four had died from falls, nineteen in hot springs, seven from avalanches, and two from bison.

A fatality in Pelican Creek Valley in 1984 forced experienced rangers to reevaluate their basic beliefs about grizzly bears. Years later, when we skied to the Pelican backcountry cabin for a weekend outing, Terry and I read in the cabin journal about the rangers' day-to-day reactions to the death of a young woman from Switzerland. Unlike Tesinsky, Brigitta Fredenhagen apparently had done everything right. She had suspended her food twelve feet above the ground in a tree and thirty yards away from her tent to reduce food odors. She wasn't menstruating.

Brigitta's brother told the rangers when she did not show up as planned at the trailhead after her solo trip. When Ranger Mark Marschall arrived at the scene, he found her tent with rip marks in it, a piece of scalp with hair, and bear scat with a "rubbery substance" (presumably muscle tissue) in it. Finally he found the body, what was left of it. It appeared her only offense was being at the wrong place at the wrong time. The bear killed her, and even more unsettling, the bear ate her. Some of the investigators speculated the bear actually stalked the small woman traveling by herself. They never determined for sure which bear was responsible.

Before he saw Fredenhagen's body, Mark wrote that he had always felt only reverence for the great bear. Suddenly, he wanted revenge. Yellowstone's teeth had sunk deeply into his psyche. Could bears and people use the same areas safely? Brigitta's death forced rangers who had lived in grizzly country for many years to reevaluate their confidence in this concept. One of the rangers wrote in the cabin journal, "Another name is added to the list of those who 'respect' Yellowstone—mine." Most everyone who had lived in Yellowstone knew what he meant. Ranger Jerry Mernin said this was the first truly predatory grizzly he had known about in more than thirty years of working among the great bears.

Visitors often treated Yellowstone as a giant zoo. When I worked as an interpretive ranger, I tried to convey the difference.

One day a camper rushed up to me in my ranger uniform and said excitedly, "There is a buffalo near my tent in Bridge Bay Campground!" I replied, "Yes, that is right. They live there. Be very careful." I struggled daily to find a balance between giving muted cautionary advice and terrifying people with tales of dangerous animals. Some arrived too frightened to venture far from their cars. Others grilled us for ideas on how they could meet a grizzly face to face. They seemed to long for the adrenaline rush of terror. I could understand that. Winston Churchill said, "Nothing in life is so exhilarating as to be shot at without result." Yellowstone was one of the few places where a person could still feel so fully alive.

I felt infuriated by those who openly sought bear encounters. One man bragged to me about cooking steak to bait bears near Pelican Valley in hopes of taking better photographs. As Tesinsky demonstrated, the stakes were higher in Yellowstone than for more prosaic adventures, such as bungee jumping. A bear may have died as a result of Tesinsky's hunger for an outstanding grizzly photograph. If my pedantic words made no impression, sometimes I wished the thrill seekers could read the rangers' journal about Brigitta's death. Maybe they would learn about respecting Yellowstone through the rangers' agonized soul searching.

Forced to deal too often with the grisly effects of poor judgment, the staff at the Lake Hospital developed a dark sense of humor. Each spring, they competed to guess the date of the first person gored by a bison. One year, their staff t-shirt read, "A message to the traveler from Yellowstone Park Medical Services. You have every right to indulge yourself in Yellowstone. So feed the bears, pet the moose, let your children ride the buffalo, swim in the boiling hot mineral pools, drive fast, and pass on curves. These messages from the folks who really care. Yellowstone Park Medical Services. We Want Your Business!"

We all sought humor where we could. Watching Ranger Mark Marschall try to keep a crowd of people away from a grizzly near the road, Terry told him, "It sure would be embarrassing if she charged and mauled a visitor with all these people watching." Horrified, Mark said, "I would jump in front of her and sacrifice myself, just to avoid all that paperwork." Mark was partially serious: He would prefer to rappel down a rope from a helicopter or battle six-foot waves on Yellowstone Lake rather than tackle a mountain of government forms.

In November 1986, when Sarge and I were under house arrest because of the renegade bear, I thought about Tesinsky's and Fredenhagen's fates, and I felt foolish for resenting the restrictions on my skiing, especially since one ranger figured the bear might be the same one that killed the Swiss woman. Each day, we listened to the park radio traffic about Bear 83. Before moving to our area from Pelican Valley, Bear 83 had charged several visitors and sent them scrambling up trees, forcing rangers to close hiking there. Habituated and not afraid of humans, she was a ferocious, fearless bear.

Ranger Jerry Mernin didn't like giving names to bears; it perpetuated the myth of bears being cuddly, cute, teddy bears, but I nicknamed the nineteen-year-old Bear 83 "Granny" when I learned about all the problem bears who were her progeny. She and one of her cubs broke into Bob and Alice Rollers' trailer years ago. Apparently she had been attracted to the lake area by a grease pit at the hotel, left open by a plumber from Mammoth. Some people said when 83 was a cub, she and her mother found an open grease pit there, so for eighteen years Bear 83 came back at the same time, remembering. Finding the delectable grease accessible again after all those unfruitful searches, she probably figured this was her lucky year. Researchers had proven bears have long memories about where they found food, but I didn't know if this story about Granny was true. She pried the tops off the grease pit until they were bear proofed.

Day after day we heard new reports of Granny's aggression.

She chased one of the winter keepers around and around his truck in a potentially deadly game of Ring around the Rosie. She charged the other winterkeeper on his porch. Each day the contractors called the rangers for help. Hired by a private company to remodel the Lake Hotel, the workers lived in the dormitory a quarter mile from the hotel. On the day before Thanksgiving, Ranger Jeff Henry rode his snowmobile toward the hotel to escort the contractors back to the dorm. The bear charged his roaring machine and, realizing he could not outrun her, Jeff leapt off the machine at the dorm and barely made it in the door.

Initially, headquarters wanted to leave Bear 83 alone, hoping she might hibernate soon for the winter. I felt torn. I hated the thought of her waking up on nice days all winter and harassing the contractors. Anything could happen. Selfishly, I didn't want to stay inside all winter; we had already gone a week without skiing. On the other hand, I felt sympathy for any grizzly, including this old sow and especially her cub. Grizzlies epitomized wildness for me; they were here long before we barged into their turf in Yellowstone. Finally headquarters announced its decision. The two bears would be trapped and relocated. So Terry and I spent Thanksgiving Eve in the maintenance garage, cutting up road kill to use as bait. As we started work on the carcasses, the contractors called in a panic. "The bear is trying to get into the cook shack! She's clawing at our door!" Hume, Ranger Alice, and Ranger Jeff jumped into Terry's DMC groomer and roared out of the garage. Terry's stomach turned, thinking of the engine damage from the jackrabbit start without warming up first.

My own stomach threatened to respond to the stench of our project, preparing Granny's Thanksgiving dinner. The female elk carcass wasn't bad; it had been frozen. But the deer carcass had not been frozen or even gutted. After sitting for several days, it had inflated like a grotesque, four-legged balloon that could explode at our first cut, covering us and the garage with enough aromatic gore to attract Bear 83 plus every other bear within twenty miles. Despite my fears, the cutting operation went smoothly with no explosions.

About midnight, we tied the bait to the back of the Thiokol snowcat, and Terry pulled out to meet rangers Alice Siebecker and John Lounsbury near the hotel. I tried not to think about Terry's danger. The snowcat could only crawl at seven miles per hour. He had to drag the bait a couple of miles to the trap, and I pictured him as a pied piper, followed by a line of voracious bears and coyotes. Terry reassured me, saying Bear 83 would be intimidated by the machine, and if she tried to lunge for him in the cab, the four-foot-wide, moving track would throw her off. At least that's what he told me, and I hoped he was right.

Too worried to sleep after he disappeared into the darkness, I knocked on Chris Lilley's door, and we sat together by the park radio, listening for any drama involving our husbands and the bear. I imagined other Yellowstone wives over the decades, waiting up through interminable Yellowstone nights like this, wondering if their husbands would come home. Fortunately we had access to a park radio. I convinced myself tragedy rarely arrived when you expected it.

Chapter Nine

Bittersweet Promise

---

*The frontier woman held the family together against the physical
forces that threatened them. She knew the new country as a bitter-
sweet promise.*

—Lillian Schlissel

Women's Diaries of the Westward Journey

*W*HEN I KNOCKED ON THE DOOR OF THE SNAKE RIVER
District Ranger Station that New Year's Eve day, I was
cursing my Ski-Doo snowmachine. Although it had started (reluctantly) when I had returned from a visit to Jackson Hole, it had
broken down just ten miles up the road, forcing me to hitchhike
back to the South Entrance. It was one of my first attempts at
solo snowmobiling, and I was determined to get home in time to
spend New Year's Eve with Terry.

After fourteen years as a Yellowstone ranger's wife, Cindy
Mernin had heard such knocks on the door before. They were
rare in her early years in the park. She and her husband, Jerry,
wintered at Lake from 1971 until 1975. While the park started
grooming the roads from the south to Old Faithful about that
time, they did not groom the roads to Lake in the early 1970s,

leaving the community nearly inaccessible. Ten- to twelve-foot drifts and untracked, bottomless powder discouraged visitation.

Only a few hardy souls from Cody or Powell, Wyoming, would brave the avalanche-prone Sylvan Pass and shovel their way from the park's East Entrance to the Lake area. Knowing what Sylvan was like to snowmobile in modern times—with grooming—I could not imagine risking my life as they did, trying to dig a track below the avalanche chutes.

At Lake, Cindy's community consisted of herself and three other people—her husband, Jerry, and two winterkeepers. The winterkeepers' job was to shovel roofs for the concession that operated hotels and lodges in the park at the time, the Yellowstone Park Company. When someone did knock back then, it often meant trouble. She and Jerry lived in the back of the Lake Ranger Station. Visitors carried their own gasoline, shovels, and tool kits; they coped with most problems themselves rather than looking to the park service for help. But when an avalanche on Sylvan Pass trapped a group in the park one time, they were forced to seek assistance. They stayed with the Mernins for several days, unexpectedly drawing down their food supplies.

By the time I met them, the Mernins lived at the South Entrance to Yellowstone where Jerry was the district ranger. Their home still housed the ranger station, which meant the snowmobiles lined up in their front yard. Although they were sixty-four miles from the nearest town—Jackson, Wyoming—they had much more access to the outside world than they had when they lived at Lake. They had to snowmobile only three miles to reach their cars, parked for the winter at the Flagg Ranch, a tourist facility between Grand Teton and Yellowstone national parks. With the advantages of being so close to civilization, they had to endure the constant roar of snowmobile traffic, the asphyxiating fumes—and more knocks on the door.

I had never met Cindy, but I stopped worrying as soon as

she answered the door that New Year's Eve. Learning that I was a park service wife, her scowl evaporated. She had little tolerance for most modern visitors' petty problems compared with the self-reliance of visitors in the old days. The night before my visit, two visitors ran out of gas and insisted that it was the park's fault. Cindy became especially irate at visitors who furtively pissed in her front yard and one who actually defecated there.

A registered nurse by training, she radiated confidence, which must have comforted many patients with worse problems than mine. Jerry wasn't home, but she would fix the machine and get me back to Lake for New Year's Eve, she told me. After she diagnosed my machine, however, she said I wasn't going anywhere. The clutch was out, and Terry would have to order parts. Terry was working and could not retrieve me and the machine until the next day. Thus it became the first of many evenings spent at the Mernins' home over the coming years, trading stories.

Cindy and Jerry had taught themselves the basics about repairing snowmobiles out of necessity. Jerry first lived at Lake in 1968. Back in the 1960s and 1970s, snowmachines were even more temperamental, and they couldn't depend upon hitching a ride with a passerby, as I had. There weren't any. With the snowmobile manual close at hand, Cindy spent hours in the shed working on their private machine, tearing down the clutch or the carburetor and putting it back together. She figured they spent four hours on maintenance for every hour they rode their 440 Ski-Doos. Despite their precautions, they invariably were miles from home when the drive belt broke or the fuel filter needed to be dried, with bitter cold stiffening their bare hands and sometimes a bison pacing menacingly nearby.

Before she arrived at Yellowstone, Cindy had never seen a snowmobile. She grew up in the suburbs of Baltimore, running almost feral with her siblings in the woods surrounding their home. One fateful day, Cindy and two nurse friends decided to seek adventure. Cindy favored the Amazon where it would be warm. Kathy and Leslie disagreed. Shutting their eyes, they pointed to a map of the United States and randomly chose a destination where they would apply for nursing jobs. Cindy's destiny lay at their fingertips. The seasonal hospital at Yellowstone Lake agreed to hire all three would-be adventurers for the summer, and they headed west for what they thought would be a short detour in their lives' direction.

When they arrived at Lake, the first person they met was Ranger Jerry Mernin. Cindy recalls how well composed he was in his appearance, his speech, and his focus. He courted the young nurse that summer and nearly fell out of his chair at her outrageous humor. When the Lake Hospital closed for the season and she prepared to return to Baltimore, he proposed. In December, she returned to Montana and they were married. The next day, she climbed onto a snowmobile for the first time and helped Jerry pack all her possessions—including her Mix Master—in the sled behind. It was a big snow year, even for Yellowstone, and she caught glimpses of abandoned snow coaches on the side of the road. Their arduous, forty-nine-mile, two-day trip made my trips in and out of the park seem like a drive to the mall. In the middle of Hayden Valley, she listened in disbelief as her husband of three days swore, struggling to convince their Ski-doo to pull their sled through unpacked drifts. An outwardly calm man, accustomed to typical Yellowstone crises, Jerry was much less likely to swear than she was.

The exasperating day would have tried the patience of a saint, much less a bridegroom trying to convince his bride that Yellowstone was a hospitable place. Not only did the sled carry Cindy's belongings but also lugged Jerry's tent, sleeping bags, and skis. Jerry wanted to be prepared: If his gentle coaxing didn't keep the machines moving, they would have to spend the night in a snow bank. Each time they encountered a difficult drift, he unhooked the sled and ran the snowmachine ahead to make a track. Circling back (the machines had no reverse), he would take his sheepskin mittens off, reattach the sled, and try again.

The swearing erupted when the machine's engine died for no apparent reason. In those days, Jerry wore a rubber slicker over his wool clothing in an attempt to keep dry. Lightweight, water repellent materials such as Gore-tex and polypropylene had not been invented, or at least they hadn't yet migrated into the wilds of Yellowstone. The snowmachine carburetor on the old machine was exposed, so when Jerry leaned forward for the final push, his jacket fell against the air intake, snuffing the engine.

They arrived at Lake exhausted, but they didn't have to sleep in a snow bank. To Cindy, the trip was a grand adventure, and she couldn't wait to tell someone about it. But who was there to tell? The two winterkeepers—Jerry Bateson and Joe Soucek—were friendly but taciturn. From 1950 to 1975, Jerry Bateson wintered at Lake, a lifestyle that did not attract the loquacious. He would check in each day to tell the Mernins that he and Joe were okay; they hadn't fallen off a roof. Although they used safety lines and creepers (contraptions with teeth that strapped on their boots for traction), the work was dangerous, and they each worked alone. Jerry Bateson was responsible for the Yellowstone Lake Hotel and several other buildings in the Lake and West Thumb areas. He worked on the steeply sloped, ice-coated hotel roof, four stories above the ground. He might listen to Cindy's story, but she sensed he wouldn't be impressed by her little adventure.

Joe Soucek was even less outgoing than Jerry Bateson. He left it to Jerry to make the obligatory daily report. His fellow workers during the summer called him "Silent Joe." According to local legend, callers during the summer were sometimes bewildered when he answered the maintenance shop telephone with his typical smile and silent nod. To prepare for his confinement at Lake, Joe shaved his head each fall so he wouldn't have to go out of the park at all, Jerry Bateson told us. At that time, the Yellowstone Park Company supplied food for its winterkeepers. Jerry ordered a side of beef, a ham, and vegetables in huge, number ten cans for himself, his wife, and his son. But Joe just ordered enough sandwiches to last him five or six months.

Cindy's fellow nurse adventurers, Kathy and Leslie, of course, had demanded that she write them letters about her first winter in Yellowstone; they wanted to read the latest chapter of the adventure. But after she wrote the letters, she couldn't mail them until Jerry went out for groceries several weeks later. For the first time in her life, her days weren't structured around work or school. A nursing job was not an option during the winters—not unless she lived separately from her husband on the outside, as did some of the wives in later years. Jerry was out on patrol much of each day, trying to keep at least a single snowmobile track open, monitoring the wildlife, measuring snow depths and moisture content, and shoveling roofs of the government buildings.

Once each winter, other rangers would come from Mammoth for an annual ski trip into the Yellowstone backcountry. Jerry would ski off with them across the frozen lake, leaving Cindy for ten days to two weeks. Sometimes their friend, Mary Meagher, would come down to stay with Cindy, and the two of them would shovel the ranger station roof and other government buildings if necessary. Meagher was a researcher with the park's Resource Management Division, and her specialty was bison. In fact, her doctoral dissertation had focused on Yellowstone's bison, so she was eager for the opportunity to stay in the park interior. Cindy wore men's clothes purchased from the Army Surplus. After any exertion, the rubberized nylon pants and jackets would get Jerry and Cindy wet from sweat, making them even more vulnerable to the cold. No one wore helmets. Nor did they have any of the special coverings for their faces that we enjoyed in the 1980s.

As we got to know each other, Cindy talked animatedly with

me about the old days while Jerry wandered in and out of the dining room, responding to park radio messages and occasionally adding a comment. I relaxed into my change of plans, recognizing that once again bad luck had turned good for me. Cindy and Jerry provided my first opportunity to see how much more civilized life in the park's interior had become. I felt foolish for whining about our minor inconveniences at Lake. Jerry excused himself at 8 P.M. Despite its being New Year's Eve, Jerry went to bed at his regular time. The holiday meant little to him except the possibility of more drunk snowmobilers on the road and sleep interrupted by accidents.

I had heard about Jerry before my arrival at their doorstep. Jerry was a legend in the park and consequently a little intimidating at first. His voice was immediately recognizable on the radio—deep, calm, and professional, regardless of the emergency. Starting in Yosemite National Park as a ranger in 1956, he had worked in Yellowstone longer than any other rangers still there. He was known as a ranger of the old school, happiest in the backcountry with a string of horses rather than playing traffic cop for snowmobilers. He packed mules competently and confronted grizzlies coolly.

As he and Cindy had bantered earlier in the evening, I caught a glimpse of a warm, loving man, a man worth following into the winter wilderness, no matter what the sacrifice. When we were talking about nursing, he said, "When Cindy speaks of medical matters, listen. If she had lived in New England, she might have been burned as a witch." When the subject turned to her love for wildlife, he said, "The damn birds would follow her. Here's that chick who puts the peanut butter out."

Jerry had to work the next day, but Cindy and I weren't ready to turn in. We savored the opportunity to trade stories and nourish our new friendship, so we returned to stories about life at Lake. With all the solitude, Yellowstone's wild creatures became

Cindy's companions and her entertainment. After she learned to ski, she took the "social register" each day, the pile of feathers or the spot of blood that revealed who ate whom. One day when she was skiing, a lynx suddenly leaped into her path. She realized he had been watching her for some time. "I was awestruck by his beauty and grace, but then I wondered, what kind of situation am I in?" She turned and skied back home. She learned to check in with Jerry Bateson if she went skiing when her husband was away. "We watched out for each other."

Opening her photo album at the dining table, she introduced me to her companions at Lake in those days. An old, disheveled raven was the most regular visitor at the bird feeder. Quoth He, she called him. The old bird stood on the coal box, his feet spread for balance. One day Quoth He showed up with a sleek, younger raven. For weeks he preened on the coal box, puffing out his feathers and looking about twenty years younger. Cindy felt certain the younger bird must be a female. But one day she got fishing line tangled around her feet; the Mernins couldn't catch her to cut it off. Inevitably, she vanished; the line probably became snagged in a tree somewhere. Her loyal beau—Quoth He—disappeared for about a week, apparently staying by her side. When he came back, he looked like a forlorn, old man. That fall, he left, never to return again. Cindy says he died of heartbreak.

In another photo, an ermine had crawled into the bird feeder, his black eyes shining out of his white fur, eager for any kind of handout instead of the elusive mice that were his regular diet. When we lived at Lake in the 1980s, we rarely saw evidence of an ermine, the snow-colored night traveler otherwise known as a shorttail weasel. For one winter, however, this ermine lived at the Lake Ranger Station. Where the two wings of the ranger station/residence met, a huge icefall formed in the corner, stretching from the roof to the ground. The ermine lived behind it, sharing the hole with a squirrel, several pine martens, and a skunk. Cindy figured some lived in the attic and some underneath the building, but she never could figure out how the natural enemies coexisted without eating one another. "Necessity and politics make for strange bedfellows," she said.

Cindy cherished holidays. On Christmas and other special occasions, she invited the two winterkeepers to dinner. Cindy's culinary skills were well known when we arrived at the park, so I knew how the two men must have relished her meals over their normal fare. Although Cindy had to adapt her cooking to primarily canned foods, dinner was a treasured treat for everyone. The first Christmas, she strung popcorn and cranberries in the spruce tree outside. They had no other Christmas decorations, and she had always made the chains for the birds back in Baltimore. The birds at Lake, however, weren't accustomed to the fare. The red and white chains remained festooned on the trees for several days. Then one morning, she discovered the snow tramped down around the tree and up one side. A coyote had crawled into the tree for his Christmas feast.

The second winter, they tied the turkey carcass to the bird feeder, sure by then that the grizzlies were safely hibernating. The birds and animals pecked at the turkey carcass for hours until finally a marten pulled it loose and tried to drag it through the long, icy hole. It didn't fit, but over several more hours, he managed to break the carcass into manageable pieces. In the middle of the night, they awakened to the screams of martens, fighting over dinner. Jerry Bateson also fed the animals, letting a favorite marten drink from a saucer of milk. A coyote attacked Jerry one year, however, and the bites on his face required twenty-one stitches and fourteen days of shots. It wasn't clear whether the coyote had become too accustomed to people by being fed. Years later, his son Jerry Bateson, Jr., published a book about his father's experiences, including a gruesome photo of his father's bites.

By the time we moved to the park, regulations prohibited

feeding animals; even bird feeders were controversial. The park service wanted animals to make an honest living, consuming this-tle and marmots instead of potato chips and bread. More impor-tantly, the park didn't want the animals to associate people with food. During one of our first years in the park, we couldn't believe it when we heard that a coyote attacked a man in the north part of the park. It turned out that the man fried foods all day at the café, and his clothing had absorbed all those smells, and that coyote had been fed by tourists. Back in the 1970s, with few visitors and even fewer human residents, there was less need for regulations. The Mernins knew as well as anyone the need to avoid attracting grizzlies. One fall, a grizzly sow tore the wall off their porch while they slept a few feet away, but that story had to wait for another day.

I asked Cindy what she had enjoyed the most about her win-ters at Lake. She paused for a long time before answering. "It was radically different from anything I had ever known.... I enjoyed the closeness that Jerry and I developed during those winters..." she said. But after the initial excitement, the months dribbled on, and the novelty of their winter life faded. She realized that bats and their guano provided the only insulation in the walls. With no television or even radio, she yearned for some news from the outside world. She ran out of magazines to read and wondered why the rare visitors from headquarters did not think to bring fresh milk or their mail. When she first arrived, she wondered why Jerry had fifty pairs of underwear. Then she found out they had to pack their dirty clothing and sheets fifty-seven miles to the laundromat in Gardiner all winter. A washer and dryer were stored, unused, in a nearby building.

Her strangest, starkest memory: Shutters were nailed over all the windows. She felt as if they lived in a cave. Presumably the shutters kept the windows from breaking in and offered some protection from the cold since the windows were single-pane glass.

Did park service authorities think the glamour of their lives would sustain them and that hardship was an integral part of that glamour? Perhaps they just did not think about the districts. "Never blame on malevolence what can be explained by incompetence," Cindy would tell us, an expression that came in handy over the coming years. Jerry and Cindy had framed the iconic New Yorker cover from March 29, 1976, showing New York in some detail up to the Hudson River and then everything else an amorphous mass to the Pacific Ocean with Japan and Russia beyond. We fantasized about making our own cover, with Mammoth and its park headquarters in detail and the rest of the 2.2-million-acre park an amorphous mass.

During three summers, Cindy worked at Lake Hospital, serving one year as the head nurse. The following year she took the summer off and rode horseback all over the Yellowstone backcountry, growing to love the park and its summer face. Gradually through their winters at Lake, some of the conditions improved. The shutters were replaced with clear plastic over the windows, and the Mernins purchased their own washer and dryer. Mac Berg, a friend of Jerry's at headquarters, brought a record player, several records, and an antenna so they could tune in one radio station. Cindy taught herself to make whimsical sculptures out of rocks, wire, pinecones, and metal artifacts. Nevertheless, winter life at Lake devalued her talents as nurse, cook, and entertaining conversationalist.

Cindy wasn't the only one who found the long Yellowstone winters an incompatible bedfellow, but she may have been the most vocal about it. Cindy's husband loved Yellowstone more than anyone; studying a map of the park was a religious experience for him. Yet he accepted the fact that Cindy felt different. Hearing her describe Yellowstone winters as "brutal," some wives quietly agreed. Other Yellowstone employees—both men and women—winced as if they had been personally assaulted. How-

ever, their lives were not centered about the hearth and the home.
They came at their own volition to jobs they enjoyed and usually
lived in winter communities larger than three. Although I whined
and worried a lot, I would never have described the winters as
brutal. I remembered when Lorie and I first heard the deep moan
of the lake ice freezing. When the expanding ice could no longer
withstand the strain, it cracked at the pressure points. To me, it
sounded like a giant passing her moistened finger around the rim
of her mammoth wine glass. The Shoshone Indians must have
named Bull Lake, down on the Wind River Reservation, when
they heard a ghostly wail like this; they say a bull elk trapped beneath the ice called from the depths. I also cherished the memory
of one evening when I was skiing with Carol Shively: The moon
hung full above Fishing Bridge while swans floated, noisily trum-
peting in the mist. Then a bald eagle flew across the moon. At
moments like that, Yellowstone was a paradise, not brutal. But
unlike Cindy, I usually had friends to share those moments with.

If winterkeeper Jerry Bateson's wife, Thelma, had been alive
when Cindy arrived at Lake, it would have been a totally different experience for them both. She died of complications from
diabetes three years before Cindy arrived. Like Jerry Mernin, Jerry
Bateson remembered the Lake winters fondly, telling us, "I would
still be there if I hadn't gotten so doggone old." But as the only
woman at Lake for eighteen years, Thelma may well have shared
some of Cindy's feelings. An accomplished singer and guitar player, Thelma had toured with the USO in Europe for three years
and performed on the WLS radio program, National Barn Dance,
before she moved to Wyoming.

I tried to imagine how different the two women's experience
would have been if they had lived at Old Faithful in the 1920s.
In some ways they would have enjoyed a more civilized winter:
The winterkeepers then had a greenhouse heated by geothermal
water. Even when the temperature was fifty below, they enjoyed

moist, warm air inside, with flowers and vegetables flourishing in the sunlight.

In contrast, Thelma Bateson could not stand the cold and rarely went outside. Afraid of animals and birds, Thelma couldn't even enjoy the solace of the wildlife, as Cindy did. She spent parts of some winters outside the park. Cindy also left Lake for part of one winter and went back to school. "I needed to keep my brain alive."

As Cindy and I tired and prepared to go upstairs, my eyes wandered to the large Stan Lynde cartoons of Rick O'Shay covering most of the Mernins' dining-room wall. In the first segment, newspaper reporter Allison Dragg comes to interview Hipshot about the glamour and romance of the gunfighter's life. Hipshot tries to tell him about the hardships—no friends, no family, sleeping with one eye open, and cold camps. The reporter walks away, shaking his head sadly, saying, "Poor fellow. He certainly doesn't know much about his own profession."

Cindy remembered those early winters as a "brutal experience … I don't think anyone could understand what it was like. I wasn't chained down. But at the same time, I was just as confined." To brighten the somber mood, she added, "Paradise isn't for sissies!"

CHAPTER TEN

Half-Wild Bears, Half-Civil People

If you are lucky enough to find a way of life you love, you have to find the courage to live it.

—JOHN IRVING

*W*HEN WE FIRST MET HENRY "HANK" RAHN, HE WAS A stooped old man with the weight of his dying wife in his eyes. Carrying a box of black and white slides, he told anyone who would listen about his days of glory in the 1930s when he was known as The Man Who Fed the Bears. We met him at a reunion of Yellowstone old timers organized by the National Park Service and park concessionaire TW Services in September 1986. In addition to satisfying my own curiosity, I planned to write magazine articles about human denizens of Yellowstone in earlier years. So Terry and I attended the reunion and made arrangements for interviews.

The park alumni were as thrilled as I was about the event, and they had come from all over the country. The reunion attracted diverse people—maintenance workers, chief ranger George Baggley, waiters, rangers, spouses, naturalists, busboys, and cooks.

Many had worked in the park more than fifty years earlier, but a theme repeated itself throughout the weekend: My years in Yellowstone changed my life. One man said he cried himself to sleep every night when he first left the park. Some had remained in the Park Service and moved on to other parks; some had forgone promotions just to stay in Yellowstone for their entire careers. Several said Yellowstone was the best park, the best experience of them all. One couple said they had met each other working at Canyon Village, and they had been married for forty-nine years.

At least one had achieved stardom in Yellowstone. Hank Rahn went to work driving trucks in Yellowstone in 1936 for $4.32 a day. When he saw the garbage men feeding the bears, that job became his dream. Before long, Hank got the job, thus acquiring the lead role in the last act of Yellowstone's great bear show. The garbage men always worked in conjunction with a ranger, who talked to the crowd about the bears and tried to protect the public. A young ranger with whom he worked—Gerald Ford—later became famous for a different federal job, president of the United States, but at the time, Hank's fame in the park community easily outshone Gerald's. Hank's official job title was "garbage man," not "bear trainer" or "show man." But everyone knew that the garbage men fed the bears. At the reunion, Hank attracted a crowd when he announced an impromptu slide show about his job near Canyon Village. To him, eliminating the bear feeding was a big mistake, and his lack of scientific training didn't deter him from expressing his opinions. At the reunion, I overheard him tell one of the park's top-ranking administrators, "I think I'm going to have an argument with you tonight."

Living in Yellowstone has always meant living with bears. Most of the former employees at the reunion had their own bear stories. Between the lines, the stories conveyed lessons for new residents sorting out the park's peculiar protocols and how they have changed. Larry Powers had once lived in the park service apartment that we lived in. We had always wondered about the peculiar scratches on our back door. Larry said a grizzly had chomped into the door in frustration one day, smelling the aroma of food inside. No one locked their doors when he worked at Lake in the early 1970s. That way if someone suddenly encountered a bear, he or she could get inside quickly, Larry said.

Since the early 1900s, park managers had used the bears both to dispose of garbage and to attract more visitors. As the number of visitors increased, so did bear-caused injuries to people and bear deaths, according to Paul Schullery in his book, *The Bears of Yellowstone*. Bears lost their fear of people. Compared with running down a marmot or licking up maggots, it was much easier to swipe a sandwich out of a tent or scare a fisherman into giving up his bag of fish. Beggar bears didn't make very good neighbors. Park employees and their families learned to tell the difference between an earthquake and a bear shaking the trailer. The situation invited tragedy. By the time Hank arrived in the park in 1936, Canyon was the sole public feeding site left in the park. Anyone who wanted to watch the bear show went to Canyon. One night, there were so many cars that they had to feed twice, Hank said.

The daily ritual started when Hank and his helper collected the garbage from the Canyon Hotel and hauled it south to the giant arena at Otter Creek, where dozens of bears would be waiting impatiently. As they dumped the garbage cans for the bears, the rangers let the tourists—sometimes more than a thousand—into a cage where they could sit on logs and watch the show. The cage provided the visitors with relative safety, but the men feeding the bears were responsible for protecting themselves. Hank accepted the danger of the work. Twenty-five years old and single, he enjoyed the glamour that accompanied the risk, and undoubtedly welcomed the attention it brought from young women. When he was off duty, he would return to the feeding ground to take pictures. One night when his fiancée, Mildred Howard, accompanied him, they saw eighty-six grizzlies. Usually there were forty to fifty, he said.

As soon as he became the head feeder, Hank changed the barrier on the 1928 truck, a ton-and-a-half Chevy flatbed with only a stock rack separating the bears from the men. When the men climbed on to the truck bed each evening to dump the garbage cans, impatient bears would reach through and grab the men's legs and start to climb onto the truck bed. Hank took off the rails, leaving ten-inch boards along the bottom of the flatbed. If a bear started to reach up to get a can, Hank would knock them off with a lead-filled pick handle. The first time he hit a bear across the nose, it broke his club. After that he forged a heavy iron wagon tire around the club for added clout. When he beat bears with the reinforced club, they fell to the ground and lay stunned for several minutes. He feared that someday he might kill one, but what scared him more was the thought of striking with so much momentum that he would fall into their midst.

Often the bears would slash into each other, fighting over the garbage. To put on a better show, the men would toss a bone into the mass of growling fur to start a brawl. Once in a while, the bears would continue their fight underneath the truck, threatening to overturn it. In addition to the cuts, diseases, and worms they acquired from the other bears, the bears suffered from "hardware disease." Hank said they tried to feed them only "good, clean kitchen garbage." But occasionally, he said, the dishwashers at Canyon Hotel would let a plate, a knife, a broken glass, or an empty tin can slip into the garbage can. Bears that wolfed down such trash sometimes died from internal injuries.

One of the great tragedies of Hank's life was when he lost most of his Yellowstone photos in a flood after he left the park. Those that he salvaged were made into slides especially for the reunion. Showing his slides, Hank pointed out that the bears coming out of hibernation in the spring were "thin as a rail." He believed his work helped both the bears—which became fat and sleek by the fall—and the tourists. "Everyone got a big kick out of it," he insisted. Pointing to his own picture, he said, "You can tell I'm not afraid of grizzlies." Hank acquired his courage from the belief that the bears recognized him, and he knew each of the bears and its peculiarities. He educated them with his club. When a stranger was in the truck, the bears would know it. Not everyone could take the danger. Talking with oldtimers later, we heard several stories of men who left the park service rather than face the hungry bears.

Young men taunting the fates every day naturally had some close calls. The men learned quickly to stand their ground and never run: A running person looks too much like dinner to the bears. The men's egos and their love of pranks occasionally interfered with their good sense. One evening, Hank's helper threw a bone at a sow grizzly just as Hank stepped onto the ground. The bear charged. With the bear just two feet away, Hank could see only teeth and claws. Not having enough room to open the truck door, he coiled his body and leaped, landing on his belly on top of the cab. "I don't know how I done it, but I did," he said.

During his travels around Montana fifty years later, he still met people who remembered watching him feed the bears. By allowing him to focus upon those days of glory, the reunion provided a brief respite from years devoted to nursing his wife, Mildred. Hank returned often to the park afterwards and visited us, and one year he showed up with a new light in his eyes and his new bride, Esther, at his side. Although Esther had never lived in Yellowstone, she enjoyed the visits and never seemed to tire of watching the slide shows or listening to the stories of The Man Who Fed The Bears.

I, too, enjoyed Hank and his colorful storytelling. He was a hard working, kind man, devoted to his work and justifiably proud of that. Hank's stories became favorites in our collection.

His tales and those of others we talked with helped us understand the changing policies toward wildlife over the decades—policies that, when read about in the sterile pages of a book, seemed cruel or mystifying. By the time that Hank arrived in the park, park rangers had killed all the wolves. Even pelicans were considered undesirable predators. During the 1920s, rangers stomped pelican eggs because the graceful, soaring birds ate too many fish and carried worms that threatened the fish. The Fishing Bridge Visitor Center (where I later worked) is filled with stuffed birds and mammals, many of which were killed for the exhibit that opened in 1931. Two rangers that we met through the reunion, Scotty Chapman and Bob Murphy, told us about their involvement in the vast elk reductions, when Yellowstone rangers shot hundreds of elk to reduce their impact on the habitat. Although Chapman believed he was doing the right thing, he said the rangers never hunted for pleasure after that. "We kind of lost our bloodthirstiness," he said.

When a California museum wanted a grizzly for its collection in 1943, Yellowstone administrators instructed Bob Murphy to shoot one. On his wall hangs a photo of the young ranger in uniform with the massive head of a male grizzly, the second largest ever taken in Wyoming. The bear's head dwarfs Bob, who said—in his precise way—the skull measured fourteen and one quarter inches by nineteen inches. Even on all fours, the bear must have stood nearly eye-to-eye with Bob—the bear's shoulders were four and a half feet tall. Talking about the incident with us in the 1980s, Bob said, "I was proud at the time, but now I look at it with bewilderment."

The great bear show had a heavy toll for both humans and bears. A forty-five-year-old woman was killed by a bear at the Old Faithful Campground during Hank's last year in the park—1942. The death resulted in the park paying its first "relief bill" to the family, according to Schullery, who wrote that an average of thirty-three bears were killed each year between 1931 and 1941.

With the drop in visitation during World War II, the quantity of garbage also dropped. After the war, the park continued to feed garbage to bears until 1970, but away from public view. After 1970, the park embarked upon an ambitious campaign to rid the campgrounds of all bears. Trapping and relocating bears became a hair-raising, around-the-clock job for rangers, especially in the Lake area where Jerry Mernin was stationed. In his own memoir, Jerry lamented that the park had to destroy so many bears because of conflicts with humans. Yellowstone did not start using bear-proof garbage cans until tragic events in Glacier National Park in 1967 forced them to respond: Two young women were killed by bears in one night, bears that had been habituated to humans by eating garbage. This tragedy was chronicled in Jack Olsen's book, *Night of the Grizzlies*.

Jerry was known for his cool professionalism in handling bears. Francis "Red" Payne, a road foreman at Lake, told us Jerry always gave a bear the benefit of the doubt. Jerry knew that bears often bluffed. Watching a bear charge toward him, he would wait until the last possible moment to shoot. "He wouldn't shoot unless they were brushing the buttons off his shirt," Red said. But one of Jerry's bear stories puts him in a slightly different light. While accustomed to bear encounters, he did not want a grizzly in his bedroom. Jerry and Cindy's apartment was in the same building as the ranger station, separated only by a porch. It was 2 A.M. when Cindy felt the cabin shaking like a semitrailer on a rough road. She nudged Jerry, who jolted awake, remembering the sow grizzly that had been searching for garbage at the trash incinerator. Their voices alarmed the bear, which rammed the window. Knowing that the tranquilizer gun was inaccessible in the ranger station, Jerry reached for his .44 magnum and the telephone, calling another ranger to drive over and scare the bear away. As the bear rammed the window again, it bulged toward them, but miraculously the window did not break.

When the other ranger arrived and retrieved the tranquilizer gun, the bear disappeared. But not for long. At 4 A.M., the bear ripped through a wall of the porch. By that time, Cindy was fully clothed, with her stocking cap yanked over her ears, puffing on her cigarette, ready to evacuate if the bear broke through. (I didn't ask her if she had written her will as I had when facing a much more mundane threat on Sylvan Pass.) By then Jerry, too, had dressed. Rangers have to catch sleep when they can, however, so he had climbed back into bed and fallen into an uneasy slumber when suddenly Cindy yelped. Leaping out of bed, he grabbed the .44 with one hand and the flashlight with the other. He was ready for anything, anything but his wife's explanation: She had sat on the icy porcelain toilet without benefit of the seat. Jerry swore he never again left a toilet seat up—even in a men's room. No records were kept about the words exchanged at that moment. At 6 A.M. the grizzly pressed her snout against the window, and Jerry shot her with the tranquilizer gun. She and her cub were relocated, and that adventure was over.

By the time we arrived in the park, its animals were allowed to be wild. The park did not try to manage their numbers or civilize them. The bears had to make an honest living rather than begging for their supper at the roadside. By 1970, bear-proof cans had been installed in all the campgrounds, and people like Lorie Rippley collected garbage every day and trucked it out of the park. As a result, bears rarely visited campgrounds or residential areas.

But the solution was not perfect. Yellowstone was not a zoo with bars separating animals from people. Nor did the animals live as they could before the arrival of the white man nearly 200 years before. Photographers still groped for the glory that proximity to the great bear could bring, getting much too close. The bear show was over, and Hank deeply lamented the park's decision to stop feeding the bears. He had stood between the preeminent symbol of wildness—the grizzly bear—and a symbol of the downside of "civilization"—human garbage. He often said it was a lot easier to educate bears than to teach people. People in and around the park continued to argue about how best to mix civilization and wildness. The perspective of Yellowstone's residents continued to be tempered by reality. Living in close proximity to such wild neighbors eliminated easy sentiments. Life at the interface—between wilderness and civilization—challenged both the critters and the community.

CHAPTER ELEVEN

Creating a Home on the Range

The frontier is not necessarily a fixed time or place. It's a way of life.
Frontiers pass, but they endure in their people.

—HAL BORLAND, *HIGH, WIDE, AND LONESOME*

*W*E FIRST NOTICED BOB MURPHY AT THE REUNION WHEN we heard him interjecting dates and numbers into other oldtimers' less precise stories. Indeed, Bob Murphy had what Westerners call a steel-trap mind. He had worked as chief ranger and superintendent at several different parks, but he and his wife returned to Montana to retire. Despite his sixty-eight years, he still had the wiry figure of a man who had spent his life working hard outside, not behind a desk. When Terry and I interviewed him, Bob told us stories about the hundreds of miles he had skied in the Yellowstone backcountry in the 1950s, his involvement in rounding up bison at the Buffalo Ranch, and the record-breaking grizzly that he had shot, all evidence of a different era in park management. As fascinated as we were by his stories, we knew that many people interviewed rangers—and Bob in particular. He had written his own books about his experiences. So I wanted to

talk to his wife, Alice. As we got to know them over several interviews, Alice was gracious, apparently feeling a sisterhood with
the new generation of park interior women. But she could not
imagine why I would want to interview her. Bob was the one who
remembered the dates and the numbers.

Talking with the Mernins and reading books about pioneer
women of the western frontier had ignited my curiosity about Yellowstone's pioneers. Historian Glenda Riley (*The Female Frontier:
A Comparative View of Women on the Prairie and the Plains*) and
others found that on the western frontier in the 1800s, women's
attitudes varied vastly from one another. Some followed their
husbands or fathers reluctantly, leaving behind their families,
churches, homes, pianos, and gardens. In other cases, the women
initiated the migration for their families out of economic necessity, a thirst for adventure, or because they chafed at women's
roles in the genteel societies back home. A number of them set out
on their own, most notably the Mormon converts who walked
toward Salt Lake City pulling handcarts. Some single women filed
for and proved up on their own homesteads.

The young and those who grew up on farms and ranches
adapted more easily. A few of the pioneer women collapsed physi-
cally and psychologically. Often they found a measure of satisfaction in their new lives and even preferred their lives on the
frontier. Just as they did, we women in Yellowstone reacted differently, depending upon our health, our childhood experiences, our
work, our husbands (if we had them), and our favored pastimes.
Other than me, Lois Lounsbury seemed to be the only spouse of a
working man at Lake who liked the winter. Lois met her husband,
Ranger John Lounsbury, when she was a fire lookout. They even
liked camping in the snow, an experience I had endured in the
past but not really enjoyed.

In the historical accounts of the western frontier, the men,
almost without exception, focused on accomplishments. Wom-

en were more likely to note the cost of the journey—the babies buried along the trail, the dust, the drownings, and the deaths in childbirth, according to Riley and other historians. That was certainly true of Cindy Mernin. Her starkest memory was the shutters nailed over the windows, but her husband Jerry did not even remember the shutters until reminded of them. Later I asked him, "Are women more conscious of comfort than men?" I felt uncomfortable even framing the question in gender terms. We discussed various individuals we knew at Yellowstone, both men and women, who did not fit into that mold. Jerry was known as someone who mentored female rangers and supported their careers. He didn't consider it a gender issue. A well-educated and well-read man (he graduated from the University of Notre Dame and attended law school), Jerry readily participated in such philosophical discussions. Drawing upon his knowledge of military history, he said support troops who provided meals and medical help during the wars noticed discomfort and deprivation more than the soldiers they were supporting. The comparison seemed apt to me; both park service wives and support troops were trying to create comfort for others.

I wanted to know more about Yellowstone's pioneer wives— their dreams, their most gratifying moments, and the cost of their journeys. Alice Bigelow and Bob Murphy met in Yellowstone in 1943 when she worked in the chief ranger's office. At that time, a woman who wanted to live in the wilderness married a ranger; women were rarely hired as rangers themselves except during World War II when there were not enough men to work. Nothing made Alice happier than accompanying Bob on horseback on trail-clearing trips into the Yellowstone backcountry, where she was responsible for catching, cleaning, and cooking the fish. Alice had worked her way up through various administrative jobs around the country, yet her favorite seemed to have been chief angler and camp cook in Yellowstone. Subsequent decades added a few inches to her girth and a few creaks to her body that made it more difficult for her to swing into a saddle, and her feet suffered from wearing pointed-toe cowboy boots all those years. She joked that she had more boots than Imelda Marcos had shoes.

To make Alice feel more comfortable with her taped interview, Bob provided his wife with a written list, including her birthday, wedding day, and dates for each move to a new park. But her stories interested me the most when they strayed into the day-to-day details about the frustrations and joys faced by families in the wintry Yellowstone wilderness.

Her love for the outdoors was given a difficult test in 1952-1953, the only winter they spent together in Yellowstone's backcountry. Just before Christmas, the chief ranger told Bob he was being transferred from a front-country position to the isolated Snake River Ranger Station at the South Entrance of Yellowstone. During the winter, rangers at that station provided critical protection from poachers, monitored wildlife, and shoveled buildings overloaded with snow.

Normally, rangers were told about their winter assignments several months ahead so they could stock up on supplies and acquire the mindset necessary for being snowed in for a long Yellowstone winter. However, the Murphys had only one-week's notice; the previously designated Snake River ranger was chosen for another job at the last minute. Since Bob and Alice had no children, Bob was tasked with the remote winter job. Rather than dwelling on the inequity, Bob and Alice dashed to Bozeman, Montana, buying and wrapping all their Christmas presents and leaving them with her folks in Gardiner to deliver, visiting his father at the hospital, and trying to imagine everything they might need for the coming months. On impulse, they bought a sewing machine so Alice would have something to do. They bought cases of cigarettes but not much food. Instead, they were expected to pay the departing ranger $1,000 for the food he and his wife had stocked for themselves.

Families everywhere know how their buying and eating habits differ from others'. When Alice arrived at their wilderness outpost and surveyed the shelves of food, she saw rows and rows of cereal boxes and canned goods that the Murphys never would have chosen for themselves. The previous ranger's family had hung paper bags full of fresh tomatoes from the ceiling; buried carrots, rutabagas, and celery in sand in the basement; and layered eggs—sixty dozen!—in galvanized garbage cans with oats as packing material. The Murphys brought some of their own meat. They didn't need a freezer; they hung it in the unheated shed.

Their small kerosene refrigerator wouldn't hold much; fresh fruit and vegetables would not be part of their winter diet. A generator produced electricity a few hours a day for vacuuming and running the washing machine. (Commercial electricity didn't come to most of the park until 1958—six years later.)

Alice's story made me feel unbelievably lucky to have a full-sized refrigerator and cupboards full of food that we had chosen for ourselves. We enjoyed good FM radio reception, and with the help of a booster and an antenna, we could get National Public Radio from Rexburg, Idaho. When the commercial power went out, our community had a large generator. It was Terry's least favorite job, taking his turn babysitting the generator. Probably left over from a World War II Navy ship, the old electrical coils looked like they came from Frankenstein's laboratory. It was noisy, smelly, and dangerous—sparks would fly when he pulled the main switch, but at least we were never out of electricity for long.

Alice said she really didn't mind the inconveniences of storing food without commercial electricity. Raised on a Montana ranch, she had not been brought up to be a whiner. But forty years later when I talked with her, she still remembered her new neighbor's rude greeting. The Snake River Ranger Station was in a two-story house, divided in half vertically except for the shared basement. It was the same duplex/ranger station where I first met the Mernins. At the time the Murphys lived there, however, it was much more isolated: The plows stopped at Moran, Wyoming, twenty-five miles south of the park entrance. The other ranger assigned to the Snake River Station, Bob Jones, and his wife and children, were the Murphys' only neighbors.

Forced togetherness with no reprieve can be difficult even for a man and woman who have chosen to spend their lives together, and even more so for strangers who are flung together by the fates. Pat's first words to Alice were, "We were hoping for someone with children." Startled but resilient, Alice replied, "Well, Pat, we didn't ask to come here either, but we better try to get along because it's going to be a long winter." It was to be a long winter, longer than either of them imagined. The plows did not arrive until May 23—five and a half months later. The winter challenged even Alice's and Bob's resilience.

I felt shocked by Pat's rude comment. At the same time, I could imagine Pat's apprehension. Even with our Lake community of twelve, we felt uneasy about newcomers disrupting the dynamics. Community spirit is a fragile thing. The smaller the community, the greater its fragility. Everyone seemed to get crotchety in the fall; anticipating the long winter was always worse than the experience itself. Of course Pat preferred having the previous ranger's children there. Keeping two boys (a two-year-old and a five-year-old) entertained without any other children around must have been challenging.

During the first couple of months, the men took turns retrieving the mail from the Moran Post Office, a ski trip that took two days. In February, the Murphys bought a snow plane. Resting on three skis and powered by an airplane engine and a pusher propeller, the snow plane could carry two people. With the snow plane the mail run became an easy, two-hour trip—when the snow conditions were right. Over-the-snow tracked vehicles had only recently been invented, and neither snow coaches nor personal snow machines (such as those used by the Mernins) were used in the park until later.

The snow plane offered an important outlet for the two families. The winter's forced intimacy would have gnawed on the best of friends. The Murphys knew their neighbors' habits all too well. The Joneses slept late, and Alice's cigarettes kept disappearing. Bob Jones insisted he had quit smoking, but after she went to bed, she would hear the refrigerator door opening in their shared basement. Although experiencing a far from a traditional lifestyle, the women spent much of their time on traditional chores, utilizing the technology of their parents' generation—wood stoves for cooking and stove-heated flat irons for pressing clothes. The men usually took care of the heavier work, hauling coal for the furnace and kerosene for the refrigerator, starting the generator, and splitting wood. Despite Pat's and Alice's mutual misgivings, they found some common interests and gradually adjusted to the interdependence. Both Catholics, they shared fish dinners on Friday nights, dressing up to go next door. When the men were gone, Pat invited Alice to share meals with her and the children.

Roles were more strictly defined among men and women of that generation than mine. Men enjoyed being gallant, and women tended to appreciate the chivalry. The reality of life on the Yellowstone frontier often undermined such intentions, however. The men skied off for several days at a time, staying at backcountry cabins built for that purpose by the U.S. Army decades earlier. They monitored wildlife, measured snow depths, and watched for evidence of poaching. Pine martens were a favorite target at the time. "They could get $35 or $45 for a marten pelt, and a dollar was a lot of money," according to Bob. Once a month, backcountry rangers had to measure snow and moisture content at dozens of specified spots along snow courses in their districts. People downstream needed the information, and much of the West lies downstream from Yellowstone. The amount of snow in Yellowstone means either drought or floods for people in the Columbia and the Missouri River basins, from Idaho to Washington and from Montana to Iowa. In addition to the required duties, Bob admits they got a little "snow wacky," taking extended ski trips just for something to do. He figures he skied more than 800 miles during that one winter, using seven-and-a-half-feet long hickories—extra long and wide to accommodate the deep Yellowstone snows and consequently extra heavy.

The ski trips left Alice and Pat alone with the chores. Alice took over the outside responsibilities—hauling the coal and kerosene and splitting the wood. Because Pat had to stay with the children when the men were gone, she ran the park service radio, answering questions and taking messages from park headquarters.

They prayed there would be no emergencies with the children, miles from the nearest medical help. Death was no stranger in the Yellowstone backcountry. In 1927, a ranger naturalist died at Old Faithful when he ate water hemlock, thinking it was a different, edible plant. Anything could have happened; a grizzly bear could have broken into their bedroom. In fact, one of the Jones's boys fell off the two-story roof, but because the snow was deep, he was not seriously injured. With the kerosene refrigerator, Alice continually worried about the possibility of a fire. She had heard the previous Snake River Ranger Station/residence had been destroyed by fire when Ranger Scotty Chapman and his wife and child lived there. Bob said the men worried about something going wrong during their absence, especially during extended trips, but what choice did they have?

When we lived in the park, the rangers no longer made regular trips to backcountry cabins during the winter. Poachers rarely undertook the arduous, dangerous trips into the park to kill wildlife as they had in earlier decades: In one instance, a poacher used a helicopter to take a bighorn sheep ram on Mount Norris. Modern technology made it possible for the park to monitor wildlife from the air, and SNOTEL devices at remote locations broadcast snow moisture and depths, the broadcasts bouncing off meteor trails and back to the master computer. Occasionally rangers or other NPS employees would ski to the cabins to shovel snow off the roofs and clean up after the mice. When we did, we religiously adhered to the old park service traditions for leaving a cabin. Lois Lounsbury, Lorie Rippley, and I took the five-hour ski across the lake ice one weekend to stay at the Park Point cabin. Lois taught us the precise, time-consuming procedure. It was much more than just empty etiquette. Each visitor must leave the cabin ready for a nearly frozen person who could stumble in, grab the blankets (all hung on the rack with the folds facing away from the door), light the stove (where the tinder already has been laid) with several matches (propped handily under the stove lid). When prepared properly, the fire could be lit with one match. Ranger Jerry Mernin told us the one-match fire had saved the lives of several people, including him, in Yellowstone and Grand Teton parks.

In his retirement, Bob Murphy often would stop to visit rangers Jerry Mernin and John Lounsbury, both amateur park historians and rangers of the old school. Bob shook his head in wonder when John showed him the SNOTEL computer printout and explained that SNOTEL used meteor burst communications technology: VHF radio signals reflect off meteors many miles above the earth. John listened with envy when Bob told tales of his extended ski trips, unmolested by management for weeks at a time. Bob often told about his worst ski trip in Yellowstone. It happened during the winter he and Alice spent with the Joneses at the Snake River Ranger Station. The two men had traveled to West Thumb and Heart Lake and were ready to return home to their wives when a storm dumped more than three feet of heavy, wet snow, one of the biggest storms they had ever seen. Pat put

Chapter Twelve
Sunshine and Shadows

In the depths of winter, I finally learned that within me lay an invincible summer.

—Albert Camus

SPRING. The house trembled and groaned, releasing a quick rush of adrenalin and a reflex question, "Earthquake?" No, it was just another load of snow sliding off our roof in the afternoon sun. Opening the door at first light I heard a chorus of coyotes, moving in closer to the inhabited area. Several times that day I went outside to listen. The air smelled wet; and the snow looked dirty as the white stuff evaporated and layers upon layers of soot, dirt, pine needles, and scat consolidated into one. Finally I heard the sound we had all been waiting for—the approaching whine of the plows, our liberators. Grinning like idiots, several of us climbed on the snow banks to watch them work.

All winter we had let nature determine the height of our roadways: When it snowed, the groomer just packed it, and we rode on top. Now, after a winter of acquiescence to nature's rules, Man and his Equipment were determined to show her who was boss. The snow had been hardened by four months of compacting, so it required three different pieces of equipment. The bulldozer led the way, crawling over the top of the snow and pulling a giant wedge plow behind. Third in line came the rotary plow, churning through the snow and regurgitating a substance more like wet cement; the operator tried to avoid hitting the gawking crowd and windows with the disgorged material. As eager as the two-leggeds, bison had already passed through a cut and crowded onto the road behind the plows.

The plow operators chugged through our housing area, the maintenance shop yard, and around the mess hall where they would stay and eat during their tenure at Lake. They navigated using color-coded snow stakes inserted by Terry's crew the previous fall: Red indicated the edge of the road. Yellow for an obstacle such as a sign or a trash can. Blue, a water valve. Ruby. Ruby? Yes, there was Ruby Red Lips (the inflatable doll) beside a big sign scrawled by Lorie saying: "Welcome boys, it's been a long winter. Beer and wild women at Lake."

When the plow crew stopped work for the day, our community members piled into four-wheel drive pickups and headed north to retrieve our personal vehicles, chattering euphorically. Spring had dawdled and teased us coquettishly, pushing the mercury to 50° Fahrenheit one day and dropping to -20° the next. To us, it was no frivolous matter. Although the plows had arrived a month earlier than the previous year (March 11, 1987, compared with April 7, 1986), everyone was tired of snowmobiling. When a new rattle developed in his machine, I heard my neighbor mutter, "I HATE snowmachines!" Terry swore that if he only had a bulldozer, he would bury our balkiest machine and good riddance. Although we had never bought a new car, and our car and truck had more than 200,000 miles on them, we had learned the importance of dependable snowmachines. By then—the end of Terry's third winter—we had purchased three snowmachines (plus the one we started with), trying to avoid getting stranded again.

When we reached civilization (the tiny gateway town of Gardiner, Montana), Terry and I stayed an extra day so we could talk to William "Scotty" and Louise Chapman and learn about their years in the Yellowstone backcountry. Following our initial greetings, Terry told them with a grin, "We didn't winterkill!" The Chapmans smiled at our exuberance, but spring liberation had a different meaning to them; when they lived in the park's backcountry there were no plows, so they depended upon solar energy to gradually open the roads. Scotty had gone to work for the park service in 1930. After thirty-four years in Yellowstone, Scotty held the longevity record for the park. Scotty had given Jerry Mernin his first job in Yellowstone, as a fireguard, in 1952. (Jerry Mernin was the same age as Scotty's son, Bill.) Most of the Chapmans' contemporaries in the park were long gone. Thus the Chapmans presented a rare glimpse of early family and community life in the park's interior.

Married in 1932, the Chapmans faced many challenges raising their firstborn son, Bill, in the Yellowstone backcountry, starting before his birth. But you wouldn't know it from talking to them. By the time we met them, Scotty was eighty-one and Louise seventy-five, and more than forty years had passed since they wintered in the Yellowstone interior. Scotty described those years as a "nice, pleasant, uneventful life." I was skeptical. I had lived in Yellowstone long enough to know that their lives would have been at the least "eventful," with surely a few unpleasant moments. After all, many of those years they lived under the most isolated conditions, including four winters when their only access was by skis or snowshoes. Scotty had patrolled hundreds of miles by ski, some of it alone. What about the interminable springs after so many months of winter isolation? He seemed to have forgotten the bitter cold and the day-to-day duties that can be drudgery in any job, even glamorous ranger jobs.

I hoped for a complete, well-rounded portrayal, with both

zeniths and nadirs. But if I wanted to hear anything negative or gloomy, it was quickly apparent I was going to have to dig for it. "Didn't you have any close calls when you were out on patrol, when you thought you might not make it back?" I asked. "No," Scotty said, "Now you talk about all of this adventure stuff, but shucks, if you know how to live in the outdoors, you get along fine. You don't have any trouble." At this point, two decades after his retirement, Scotty's stories focused upon the sunshine, not the shadows. Louise had reached a point in her life where she could not fully participate in the interviews. She added a sentence or two to the old familiar stories, but otherwise, she sat quietly by Scotty's side, smiling, as he talked about their lives. In a 1978 interview with Dorothy Boyle Huyck about her work in the park during World War II, Louise was as positive and enthusiastic as Scotty was in our interview.

Terry and I immediately felt comfortable when Scotty and Louise welcomed us into their home, where they had retired on the northern boundary of Yellowstone. They were casual, relaxed, and glad to share their memories and to show their photographs. Louise reminded me of my mother. For the interview, Scotty wore an old, wool plaid shirt—no doubt one of his favorites— with a bandana tied around his neck. Scotty showed us photos of his years chasing buffalo, toting a canoe through the snow, fording the Lamar River with a full pack train, and skiing through the woods. There were lots of snow pictures. His biggest regret was losing movies from his years at the Buffalo Ranch and other photos in a house fire. Twelve years living in the Yellowstone backcountry left them unconcerned with the niceties of the modern world. I still picture a visit in late January when Scotty decided to serve us cranberry juice in Christmas mugs. In an attempt at civility, he pulled out TV trays for the refreshments, unceremoniously brushing month-old holiday crumbs onto the floor. We appreciated the hospitality.

Scotty looked like a man in his late sixties, not early eighties. When they agreed to pose outside for a photograph, we could see the dog hair coating Louise's pants, just as it always decorated our own clothing. In the sunshine we could see the purplish tinge of Scotty's nose, frostbitten one too many times. When he gripped her to his side for the photo, we glimpsed the depth of their mutual affection. The two had met in Fort Collins, Colorado, when Scotty was a student at Colorado State University (known then as Colorado Agricultural College or, in Yellowstone, as "the ranger factory"). Louise was only fourteen years old, but Scotty vowed that he would wait for her; she would be his wife. After graduating from high school, she enrolled at the university. Louise wanted to study forestry herself, but her family and her teachers discouraged her. By marrying Scotty, she got the man and the lifestyle she wanted.

In 1932, they spent their honeymoon on horseback—a two-week patrol looking for illegal hunters in the park. Louise had been raised in the city, and when ranger Joe Douglas first met her, he didn't expect the "little lady" to ever get outside the house. Louise quickly earned his respect, riding alone all over the wild country. Douglas gave her a horse as a wedding present.

Louise continued to surprise the old hands. During the fall of 1933, Scotty had left her alone at the Bechler Ranger Station when he went to fight fires for several days. Bechler was and still is one of the most isolated posts in the park. Fred Johnson, the assistant chief ranger, called the station to see if anyone could climb the fire lookout tower, and Louise answered the call. Louise knew the "fire lookout tower" was a makeshift thing, eighty feet high with boards nailed between two pine trees and a little platform at the top. She knew that it swayed back and forth in the wind. She also knew she was all alone and thus the only one who could fulfill the important assignment protecting the southwest corner of the park. So two or three times a day she climbed the tower,

This eighty-foot-high fire lookout, which consisted of boards nailed between two pine trees that swayed in the wind, was used to check for fires. Even during her pregnancy, Louise Chapman, the wife of a backcountry ranger, repeatedly climbed it. (Photo courtesy of NPS)

looked through the fire finder, and reported back to headquarters. It was years later when Fred Johnson found out that Louise had been several months pregnant at the time. According to Scotty, the assistant chief swore he would not have dared to climb the fire tower himself, "and I was not pregnant."

If she had fallen, their son Bill might never have been born. Because of the isolation at Bechler River during the winter, the Chapmans decided Louise would await the birth in Fort Collins, Colorado, with her parents. She returned in March 1933 with the three-month-old baby. The snow was just beginning to break up when Scotty strapped the baby on his back and they slogged seven miles on snowshoes to reach their home at the Bechler Ranger Station. Thus baby Bill was introduced to Yellowstone.

Like Romulus and Remus, Bill Chapman was suckled by the wilderness as he spent the remainder of his first winter and the following winter at the Bechler Ranger Station. Bechler winters always lasted six months or more, from November until the snows melted out in late May. During the day, his father was usually out patrolling on skis with his partner (Don Kipp the first winter, Tom Gary the second). They watched for signs of poachers, killed coyotes, and mapped the wildlife activity. Once every two weeks, the two men would ski fourteen miles to the nearest ranch to pick up their mail, which was delivered there by a horse-drawn sleigh. Babies usually limit their mothers' activities anywhere. We had seen our neighbors at Lake try to juggle young children with fulfilling the mothers' needs to get outside and to socialize. Although Louise had roamed alone on horseback the previous year, she had to think before venturing outside alone.

For better or worse, they had no reliable communication with the outside world, including headquarters. The phone lines usually went down early in the winter because of the heavy snow in that corner of the park, and the park radios at that time were undependable. The big radio in Mammoth would broadcast instructions to the different stations. Sometimes they would get them, but often they could not, Scotty said. If there were an emergency, they were on their own. Often he skied alone. As he talked, I thought about my own precautions. When I planned to ski alone up the steep ridge behind our house, Elephant Back, I told Terry I would tie a bandana around the dog's neck and send him home if I fell and broke my leg. Then Terry could phone or radio someone for help if necessary. Scotty had no such possibility of rescue when out alone. Even if the accident occurred at home, they may or may not have been able to notify someone. But any such worries had faded from their memories by the time of our interview.

Watching him, I could imagine Scotty as a kind, nurturing father. Their house was full of various cats and dogs they had rescued. A black, longhaired cat nuzzled into his arm while he talked. Our interview tapes were punctuated by their dog, Griz, shaking his metal dog bowl in his teeth. Regardless of Scotty's interest in being a good father back then, however, his world revolved around a different axis—work. Louise and Scotty traveled out of Bechler River together and into "civilization" only once that winter—to watch the sled dog races in Ashton, Idaho, twenty-six miles away.

Unlike Cindy Mernin, however, Louise had another woman in her tiny community for one of the Bechler winters, and the women put their creative energy together to brighten the long winter nights. Louise and Margaret Gary (Tom's wife) decided to have a formal dinner. Normally, of course, they all wore the drab, heavy, wool clothing typical for frontier winters. Stationed fourteen miles from the nearest neighbor, the women had little need for conventional clothing. For this occasion, however, they pulled their evening dresses out of storage and spent the evening dodging the wood stove with their floor-length chiffon hemlines. Scotty and Tom obliged by finding something suitable to wear.

The women fixed a special dinner. To complete the party,

the men decided to make ice cream, but there was one problem: They didn't have any rock salt. Since the nearest store was a day's travel away, they had to make do. Figuring the wintry temperature—35° below zero—might make up for the lack of salt, Scotty and Tom started cranking the ice cream maker on the front porch. Scotty wore a thick buffalo coat, but nevertheless, he still remembered, more than half a century later, the cold seeping into his bones. They cranked and cranked until finally they decided, "Nah, you can't make ice cream without salt." The evening was a highlight of their stint there, according to Scotty.

By the time of the dog races, Bill was too heavy to carry comfortably on Scotty's back. They had to snowshoe fourteen miles to reach the ranch and then ride in a horse-drawn sled the remaining twelve miles. They bundled Bill into a dog sled hitched to their old German shepherd dog, Wolf. It worked fine until the dog got sick of pulling, leaving Scotty to pull the sled the rest of the way. Baby Bill enjoyed most of the ride, even when the sled tipped and he slid off. They fed him a sandwich to keep him busy, but toward the end of the trip, he started crying, and they discovered he had lost it. Scotty had to turn back to find the sandwich, and his comment gave the only clue of the trip's difficulty. "I tell you, it was a long fifty feet to go back and get that sandwich."

Living every winter on canned food without fresh vegetables or fruit was difficult for anyone but an especially tough way to start a child. On the advice of a doctor, they later supplemented Bill's diet with vitamins. Scotty himself developed allergies to many of the foods that had been staples in the backcountry—beans and canned grapefruit juice. The backcountry life provided Bill with skills that served him well in his adult life, especially orienteering. Even as a small child, he had an uncanny sense of direction and always knew where he was in the park, according to his father. His parents would test him on it all the time. On cloudy, snowy days, when most people would feel disoriented, little Bill could point toward home unerringly.

During our second interview, we finally heard the full story of their house burning down, which Alice and Bob Murphy had mentioned to us. The Murphys were concerned because a malfunctioning kerosene refrigerator caused the fire, and they still had such a refrigerator when they lived at the Snake River Ranger Station in the 1950s. The Chapman family moved to the station at Yellowstone's south gate in 1939. Scotty was fighting forest fires elsewhere in the park when two women and their three children came to visit Louise. The children had gone to bed on the second floor when Louise smelled smoke. Working quickly by flashlight, the women grabbed the children and dragged them out of the house. Dry as tinder, the old log duplex took only fifteen minutes to burn to the ground. Keepsakes from their wedding and their first eight years of marriage, Scotty's home movies of his ranger work, and all their other belongings were gone, but thanks to the women's courage and quick action, they averted tragedy.

If young Bill were to attend school, the Chapmans could no longer live in the backcountry. So in the fall of 1940, they moved to "town"—West Yellowstone, Montana, where they spent three winters. At that time, the roads weren't plowed into West Yellowstone, and the seventy-five residents used a snowshoe trail down the middle of the street. There they could buy groceries and receive mail—whenever the horse-drawn sleigh could get through from the outside world to deliver them. In 1943 they moved to the front country at Mammoth, where Scotty spent the remainder of his career. After he grew up, their wilderness baby Bill utilized his extraordinary sense of direction as a bush pilot in the Yellowstone region. He was smaller than his two much younger brothers (Dan and Jon) who were born in 1948 and 1949 and raised in Gardiner, but just as smart, Scotty said.

Terry and I exchanged glances several times during our interviews with Scotty, both touched by the obvious bond between

Scotty and Louise and his patient efforts to include her in the conversation. Talks with Bob Murphy and Jerry Mernin also hinted at the close camaraderie they felt with their spouses. Although of course they could have—and probably did—share some harsh words over the years behind closed doors, their marriages had endured. Likewise, Louise Chapman, Cindy Mernin, and Alice Murphy not only had fulfilled their traditional roles as wives and homemakers, but also often shared their husbands' ranger duties without credit or salary.

Women of my generation tended to think of ourselves as much more independent and capable than our mothers' generation, whose lives revolved around their homes and families. My friends and I identified more with our fathers. It wasn't until after her death that I began to appreciate my mother's independence. As a young woman, before most of the Colorado ski areas had been developed, she often drove a carload of friends in her Model A Ford to ski off the top of Loveland Pass and then danced all night at Georgetown. During World War II, she served overseas with the Red Cross. Remembering that, I wanted to believe that I, too, would have climbed the Bechler fire tower and cheerfully fulfilled all the other expectations of a wilderness wife. During bad days on our modern frontier, I wondered whether I would have been a whining Cinderella instead.

The Chapmans', Murphys', and Mernins' stories hinted at a culture of rugged individualism, but symbiosis would describe the reality better. Winter residents on the Yellowstone frontier depended upon their spouses, their neighbors, and their partners. People watched out for one another. Their relationships rested on the interdependence imposed by the living conditions, not necessarily upon congeniality. They shared food, pulled other trailblazers out of jams, and traded the duty of breaking trail.

In hazardous occupations such as fire fighting, police, and ranger work, rookies pose a genuine danger to their partners when they cannot carry their share of the load. Those who held up their share earned respect and often built unexpected bonds of friendship, while those who backed out of their responsibilities failed to pass muster.

Despite spending twelve full winters in the Yellowstone backcountry, Scotty Chapman froze his feet only once—waiting for a partner who couldn't ski. Although it was fifty-six degrees below, Scotty insists he could have kept warm—if he could have kept moving. By morning, Scotty's feet had swollen so much that his ski boots had to be cut open before he could limp five miles back to the trailhead. "I couldn't walk on them for the next thirty days, and then another thirty days I wished I couldn't walk," he said. His feet still showed the scars. "If it hadn't been for that character who was with me, I wouldn't have had any trouble." He was even more disdainful of a partner who committed suicide on the other side of their duplex at West Yellowstone. "It wasn't cabin fever that did the man in," Scotty said, but "some kind of trouble he got into while on leave in California." In effect, the man had shirked his responsibilities, leaving Scotty alone to do the work of two.

Looking back over his life as a ranger, Scotty mentioned few negative experiences. Those were the good old days to him, but he admitted that West Yellowstone was "his least favorite assignment...Of all the stations, that was the most uncomfortable," he said. "I'd rather be completely isolated rather than half way like that.... If you're coming back from a big, tough ski trip, you might want to go home and sleep by the fire," he said. At Bechler, he could have slept by the fire, but at West, there might be a dance or a potluck he would have to attend. In the backcountry stations, they minimized their needs and distinguished them from desires for frills. "You knew what you want and what you need, and you got along with what you had." At West Yellowstone, however, "We were trying to live two lives—the completely wild life and then the half-civilized."

After Terry and I bade the Chapmans good bye and climbed into our truck to go back to Lake, we rehashed their stories and their significance to our modern day lives in the park interior. Scotty's comment about being half civilized gave me new perspective. Living in Yellowstone in the 1980s and 1990s, we weren't really on the frontier, just halfway there. Unlike the Chapmans, we had snowmobiles so we traveled regularly between the wilderness and the "civilized" world. The frustrations came from assuming we could get out to buy groceries, visit friends, attend a workshop, or see a concert. The week before when I had a publisher's deadline for my book, the power went out for seventeen hours and I was helpless. I wished I had my typewriter back. We depended upon having mail service and getting our credit cards paid on time. We expected many things that the Yellowstone pioneers could not have expected, but the elements often thwarted us, too. We were half-civilized.

CHAPTER THIRTEEN

Fire in the Thorofare

When autumn winds blow, not one leaf remains the way it was.

—TOGYU

*P*RIOR TO THE SUMMER OF 1988, RANGER DAVE PHILLIPS and his family found life at the Thorofare Ranger Station idyllic. Located near the southeastern boundary of Yellowstone, the backcountry station is one of the most remote habitations in the lower forty-eight states. When Phillips; his wife, Kathleen O'Leary; and his two children arrived each summer, they left the busy park highways to travel thirty-two miles by horseback into another era. Far from telephones, electricity, and the sounds of modern civilization, the Thorofare was filled with reminders of the park's earliest explorers and the reason for the area's name. Dave and Kathleen found prehistoric tools, evidence that Black-feet, Crow, and Shoshone Indians and their predecessors had utilized this route over Two Ocean Plateau near the Continental Divide and through the broad Yellowstone valley for thousands of years.

The park's wildest creatures found the Upper Yellowstone River area hospitable—with its vast meadows, wetlands, and forests. The closest road was thirty-two miles away, and only a few trails crossed the area. Unlike in areas of Yellowstone closer to roads, here the animals could go weeks without seeing any two-leggeds in the Thorofare. Moose munched on willows in the meadows, their long legs plodding through belly-deep, marshy muck. Osprey screamed from their nests when bald eagles invaded their fishing turf to dive for cutthroat trout. The prehistoric voices of the sandhill cranes emitted a Jurassic crescendo, half fear and half joy, while great blue herons silently imitated saplings in the shallows, their yellow eyes staring into the water. Grizzlies napped in the shadows of the forests, venturing out to fish or graze on thistle only when the shadows of Yellowstone's highest peaks darkened the valley.

By 1988, the frontier life seemed more natural to the Phillips family than their city lives in California, where they wintered. Tyson and Linnea Phillips started spending their summers with their father and stepmother, Kathleen, in the Thorofare in 1984, when they were nine and six years old. They grew strong at their father's side, clearing trail, repairing fences, and hauling water. I met them in 1987, and they told me about their lives at Thorofare. As with children anywhere, Tyson complained a little about his least favorite chore—hauling buckets of water from the creek—but he realized that without it, they couldn't wash dishes, cook, or clean up after a sweaty day of work. Despite the lack of running water, the Phillips enjoyed hot, outdoor showers using wood to heat the water. Wood also heated the water for the laundry, which Kathleen washed by hand. Everyone took turns feeding the horses and doing the cooking. Visitors long remembered the gourmet meals they enjoyed there.

Still young enough to enjoy "playing house," Linnea said she liked doing dishes and baking bread in the big wood-burning stove. Linnea was especially happy with the fort she built in the woods and with her trundle bed, which rolled out from under the desk in the two-room cabin. She and her brother had helped peel logs to build the bed. Without other children around, the horses, mice, and ground squirrels became her pets, and she fed them grain out of her hands. The park service employed Dave, but as often happened, it got two for the price of one: Kathleen worked as a volunteer. The children often accompanied their father and Kathleen on horseback when they visited backpackers' camps, monitored wildlife activity, or marked the park boundary with metal signs. The park needed the signs to notify hunters before they trespassed into Yellowstone during the fall hunting season. No fence separates the Bridger-Teton National Forest (where hunting is allowed) from Yellowstone National Park (where hunting is not allowed). Experienced riders, the family enjoyed their horses and looked forward to reuniting with them each summer. They couldn't imagine the horses would pose serious problems for them during the summer of 1988.

One of Kathleen's first jobs in the park was as a wrangler for the Yellowstone Park Company, which ran lodges, restaurants and activities in the park at that time. Her short, slight form looked natural in the saddle, and she could heft one easily onto the back of a horse. I heard about Kathleen's horsemanship before I met her: One day bison invaded the horse corral at Lake, the story went. Bison and horses don't mix. If a bison decides he wants grass that a horse is eating, he might hook the horse with his horns and toss it into the air. Two male rangers selected Kathleen to chase the treacherous bison out. "You can ride better, Kathleen, you do it," they suggested from the ground outside the corral. She did.

By 1988, Dave had been working in Yellowstone for twenty-one seasons. He had met Kathleen in 1983 when she went to work for the Park Service as a ranger aide. As seasonal employees, they lived in California during the winter, where Dave worked for the Dairy Council of California, taking a cow to schools to explain where milk originated. The earnest sincerity in his brilliant blue eyes could win over both skeptical schoolchildren and trespassing hunters.

Horses were essential to a ranger's work in the Thorofare, a huge, roadless portion of the park, some of it crisscrossed with fallen trees. Horses transformed long, arduous patrols into day trips, enabling Dave and his family to return home to Thorofare Station at night. Without horses, it was difficult to ford the Yellowstone River even during normal water years—sometimes waist deep on a tall person, impassable for children and small adults. In bear country, it was much safer to travel on horseback than on foot. Bears rarely charge a person on horseback. The Thorofare was definitely bear country, and the Phillips family usually saw tracks of grizzlies all summer long. Living among bears requires hyper-vigilance, never going out without peeking around the door first, keeping horse feed and human food locked up, and tuning in to every snapping twig. The children vividly recalled one night when a grizzly bear came calling at the ranger station. When Dave tapped on the window, the bear ran away.

Although the Thorofare ranger was assigned to the Lake Ranger District, we rarely saw the Phillips there. The family only occasionally took "days off" to venture to our relative civilization to use washing machines and VCRs and visit friends. Instead, they stayed in the Thorofare, usually from mid-July—when the rivers became low enough to ford safely—until late August when they returned home to California. Getting supplies could be challenging because of their remote location. It was about twenty miles by boat across Yellowstone Lake from Lake Village to the Trail Creek patrol cabin, plus another seventeen miles by trail to the Thorofare. The Phillips family always assumed that if a real emergency arose, a helicopter could evacuate a family member.

Nineteen eighty-eight began as an unusual year. Dramatically lower snow pack reduced runoff from the high mountains in the Absaroka Range. Since the streams could be forded earlier, the Phillips family rode into the Thorofare about two weeks sooner than normal. As they left, they listened casually to the report about lightning starting a fire June 23 on the west side of the park near Shoshone Lake. It seemed awfully early for fires to begin. In the West, forest fires are expected during the late summer and fall, but June?

On July 11, two weeks after they arrived at the Thorofare Ranger Station, lightning started a fire near Mink Creek, just south of them in the Bridger-Teton National Forest. The prevailing winds from the south carried whiffs of smoke into the Thorofare, only hinting at what the summer of 1988 was to bring. Kathleen's diary entries conveyed their innocence:

July 12: Another beautiful day in God's country.

July 14: The smoke has settled in—thick, sweet-smelling smoke. Linnea made a chocolate cake that took most of the evening to cook.

July 16: We got a late start back to Thorofare from Trail Creek on Saturday. I love the evening air that rolls in late in the afternoon. The kids rode ahead, and Dave and I had a lovely ride together back to the cabin. T&L had made dinner for us when we arrived.

On July 17 a helicopter invaded their tranquility. It brought a load of firefighting equipment, including a pump to be placed in the creek and a hose to run from the pump to their barn and cabin. The pump and hose looked foreign and out of place in their meadow. Kathleen wrote, "At this point, it seems impossible that the fire could actually reach here and threaten our home." Yet something was definitely strange. After so many years, the Upper Yellowstone Valley had become as familiar as their living room back in California. They had learned to predict weather by sniffing the wind and to know the changing seasons by watching the animals. During the summer of 1988, however, a cool morning that promised rain instead delivered huge cumulous clouds that boiled over Two Ocean Plateau, the clouds stained red from the fires far below, like cauliflower boiled in blood.

The wild animals acted peculiarly. Early in the summer, on a trip south to the Bridger-Teton National Forest, the Phillips noticed that trails were covered with bear tracks of every size—grizzlies' and black bears'—all headed the same direction, away from the fire. Unlike in other years, they saw no sign of bears from then on. Hawks were plentiful, more than they had ever seen. Three or four hawks at a time soared over them every day, and dove for rodents made visible by the drought-shortened grass. By late summer, a few moose and hundreds of elk herded up as if it were already autumn.

On July 22, from her front porch, Kathleen saw flames on Two Ocean Plateau. The flames burned "incredibly fast" across the face of the plateau. At 10:30 the next night, their neighbor, Forest Service ranger Ray Wilson, notified them that the fire was headed their way. After a restless night, Kathleen and the children headed for the lakeshore with nine horses, their own park service horses plus Ray's Forest Service horses. Dave stayed behind to protect the ranger station. During the tense, seventeen-mile ride, Tyson (thirteen) and Linnea (ten) proved themselves experienced hands, helping with the pack strings and clearing burned trees from the trail. For two days, they waited at the Trail Creek Cabin, fishing, drawing pictures, and monitoring the radio for reports from Dave. The smoke turned from gray to nasty brown/orange—the kind of smoke that indicates a lot of fuel burning. Their drawing papers were smudged with falling ash, but the evacuation proved unnecessary. The fire missed Thorofare so they returned home to join Dave.

After their return, the days blurred together in a smoky haze. Smoke no longer smelled sweet. After burning north to the lake along the Yellowstone River, the fires turned and burned south, against the normal prevailing wind direction. Fire roared to within a couple of miles of their ranger station and then turned again. The children understood the potential danger at a visceral level. The fire's destructive power hit home especially hard one day when they hiked up a once familiar trail, across the Yellowstone Valley. There in the blackened forest, the family found a burnt chipmunk. They stared at the tiny, charred body and then returned home. Not long after their return from Trail Creek, the children left Yellowstone as scheduled for a family reunion trip with their mother. Dave and Kathleen rode back into the Thorofare, determined to protect their home. Day after day they searched the skies for signs of rain. They found themselves cursing the lightning storms that in previous years had enthralled them.

One day while Kathleen was showering outside, two big helicopters arrived and hovered above her until she grabbed a towel and signaled to the pilots where they could find Dave. Helicopters kept arriving intermittently to bring long overdue supplies and news of fires elsewhere in the park. By August 12, park officials estimated forty-seven fires had burned over 201,000 acres in Yellowstone, and many were still burning.

It was Dave's job to protect the Thorofare Ranger Station. When it wasn't under immediate threat, the inactivity frustrated him. When they were isolated from the action, the waiting strained Dave and Kathleen's nerves as they listened to incessant fire traffic on the park radio. After each new fire report, they plotted a new escape route. As soon as each burned-out trail cooled, they cleared the burned trees out of the way, hoping the winds wouldn't shift and set it afire again. They practiced watering down the cabin with the little pumps. When they could think of nothing else to do, they painted the kitchen.

Both Kathleen and Dave were well schooled in the tradition of both ranching and the park service: Take care of your livestock first. Your horse worked for you all day, so the horse should be fed and watered before you take care of your own needs. Nevertheless, Kathleen's diary recorded growing frustration with the four horses and the mule. They were acting strangely, were difficult to catch, and escaped several times each day. "They're getting to be a real pain in the ass," she wrote on August 8. Twice that day, flames threatened the ranger station, and each time Kathleen saddled the horses and prepared to evacuate. When the threat died to an ember, she unsaddled and turned the horses back in to the pasture. Saving the horses became her day and night obsession.

Influenced by a book she was reading, *Montana's Early Day Rangers* by Bert Gildart, Kathleen dreamed she took the horses down to the river and draped them with wet blankets as the flames roared over them. She awoke every morning exhausted from lifting those heavy blankets. The book described apocalyptic fires in 1910: Wind-fanned fires killed eighty-five people, including seventy-two firefighters, and burned millions of acres. Many men died because they panicked and defied orders. One shot himself rather than face the conflagration. Another was later put in an asylum, according to Gildart.

With steep mountains all around them, the secure Thorofare Valley began to feel like a trap. Every exit route had been burned or was burning. The pumps offered some comfort. Yet watching the intensity of the fires, they began to question whether the little Mark III pumps could actually save the ranger station. Kathleen reminded herself that in 1910 they didn't have helicopters; 1988 was different. If conditions got too bad, they could call for a helicopter to lift them out. As Kathleen wiped ashes off the kitchen table, she watched herself go through the familiar motions, as if the table and the cabin would always be there.

CHAPTER FOURTEEN
The Burning Questions

We don't see things as they are; we see them as we are.

—ANAYS NIN

SEQUESTERED IN YELLOWSTONE NATIONAL PARK'S backcountry during the fire season of 1988, Dave Phillips and his wife Kathleen O'Leary had a limited window on the frenzy taking place in most of the Yellowstone front country. In the Snake River District alone, four serious fires burned simultaneously in late July. Any fire is stressful, but the administrators and firefighters normally would expect that in a few days it would be out, and they could return to their homes and families. In 1988, however, the fire nightmare continued month after month. Rangers evacuated 3,000 employees and visitors from Grant Village on July 23, and the smoke never left. Air quality monitors showed pollution equal to downtown Denver or L.A. On the front fire lines, firefighters inhaled the equivalent of four packs of cigarettes a day. Residents disconnected their smoke alarms. Terry breathed a clean sigh of relief when he returned from Grant, where he had been operating a bulldozer, clearing a fire line to protect a million-dollar microwave communication tower.

Smoke hung so thickly over parts of Yellowstone Lake that Lester Warwood had to navigate the National Park Service maintenance boat across the lake by compass. Lester knew the lake as well as anyone. For seventeen years, he had been delivering supplies to trail crews and rangers at the trailheads surrounding the lake, collecting garbage, and maintaining the outlying campsites. Each year, he monitored the lake depth. In 1988 it was the lowest he had ever seen it—six inches lower than in his previous record low.

We found humor wherever we could. When the maitre d' at the Grant Village restaurant asked whether customers wanted smoking or non-smoking, everyone always roared with laughter. Monitoring the radio, we heard Bob Mahn, a fire boss somewhere in the backcountry with poor reception, trying to be understood as he called for supplies. Known for his love of eating, he finally said in frustration, "FOOD! We need food!" Chris Lilley threatened to call an insurance company and ask about getting fire insurance. When they asked where she lived, she would cough and mutter, "Yellowstone." Maybe she would send a scorched check. We felt relatively immune at Lake. With the prevailing winds out of the southwest, the giant lake protected us in her embrace. So it was difficult for me to relate to Cindy Mernin's foreboding when she called from Snake River on July 25. The heat and dryness gave her a strange, ominous feeling. She visualized the park as a paper plate smoldering in a campfire, the brown spots slowly growing until suddenly it would burst into one grand explosion. I liked the metaphor, but it seemed a bit melodramatic. The whole park?

While the fires burned, I was obsessed with my own priorities. A publisher's looming deadline had me chained to the computer for ten hours each day trying to finish a book, despite the distractions. My computer screen glared eerily with the reflection of the sun, a dull red disk hanging in the smoke. I needed sleep to focus so I cursed when early morning phone calls jarred us awake. One night the call reported that a car had slammed into a bison obscured by the smoke. Terry had to take out the front-end loader at 3 A.M. to move the carcass before it caused another accident or attracted a bear. Near Grant Village, deer stood in the middle of the road, disoriented and staring; every week several were hit by cars. Often thunder awakened us, and we listened hopefully for the sounds of rain. But there was almost no rain that summer, only lightning. One night Lorie Rippley's telephone next door awoke us. Like many park employees, Lorie wanted to fight fires and earn extra money. To them, smoke smelled like money. Lorie's call came at 2 A.M., and she was told to be ready by 3:30 a.m. Through our shared wall, we could hear her frantic packing.

Cindy Mernin reported the chickadees were acting strange, singing their spring territorial songs at the end of July. She figured they were trying to drive off the out-of-season invasion of juncos and white-crowned sparrows that were seeking refuge from the fires. The osprey nest at Lewis Lake had burned up, she said, apparently with young birds still in it. When Lorna, our friend from Casper, Wyoming, came to visit via the South Entrance, she received a handout saying, "You are entering an area where lightning-caused fires have been allowed to burn. Your travel through the fire area is an interesting opportunity to observe Yellowstone in transition. Old forests and meadows have burned and will rejuvenate, enhancing wildlife habitat." Interesting? She couldn't believe the park would allow tourists where trees burned alongside the roads in the midst of such thick smoke. She held onto the steering wheel with one hand and used the other to hold a wet bandana over her nose and mouth to breathe.

While residents and visitors questioned the wisdom, economic interests kept the park open. When we went out to get groceries, we saw signs in Cody, Wyoming: "How natural do we have to get?" "Smoke—our tax dollars at work." "Watch the fools burn your park." At tourist-dependent Cooke City, Montana (its park access sealed off by fire), a pessimistic prankster changed the sign on the city limits to "Cooked City." Area chambers of commerce contacted state and federal officials, demanding open gates, but it seemed to us that thousands of dollars were being spent locally on firefighting. Weren't those dollars just as valuable as those of the tourists? Wyoming's U.S. Senator Malcolm Wallop responded to the pressure. He made the park service promise to keep the park open. "It is too important to the tourist industry in Wyoming and the future reputation of Yellowstone National Park to allow the park to be closed to visitors," he told reporters. We asked ourselves what would happen to the future reputation of Yellowstone if visitors got singed or burned up?

As August progressed, Cindy's paper plate kept smoldering in my mind. Could she be right? The park radios barked as in a war zone. Firefighters were pulled off one fire to fight the next before the first was fully suppressed. Helicopters and airplanes buzzed overhead, surveying fire locations and carrying firefighters and buckets of fire retardant. The pilots vied for radio time with Yellowstone's normal summer radio traffic: car collisions, people gored by bison, and backcountry camping permits. From my point of view, the distant fires seemed more meddlesome than frightening. The electricity kept going off. I backed up my files constantly but somehow each outage wiped out at least an hour's work. I found myself cursing the damn wimpy lodgepole pines for falling on the power lines after they burned. Lodgepole pines split as they grew into as many as five separate crowns. Shallow-rooted and top-heavy, they tended to be tipsy, like a fat lady on spike heels. Montana Power Company crews were working twelve- to fourteen-hour days finding downed lines and wrapping power poles in protective foil fire shelters, but they couldn't keep up. Finally they put Lake on the old generator, and the clocks gained ten minutes every twenty-four hours. That wasn't great for my computer either.

Terry's children, Sheri and Scott, had to get back to California for school, but Sheri was still working at the Hamilton Store. As they watched the daily road closures, they became more and more antsy. Their mother called to check on them after watching the television news reports about Yellowstone. We sent our golden retriever Sarge out of the park with friends for safety, but I didn't want to leave. Yellowstone was my home. In the past, during hurricanes or the Mount St. Helens eruption, I could not comprehend people who ignored evacuation orders. But as a journalist, I recognized a big story, and I didn't want to miss it, even if I didn't have time to cover it. As a wife, I wanted to be by Terry's side, not miles away speculating. I knew some wives evacuated from Grant had been gone for six weeks. Besides, I still questioned the danger as I watched others at Lake pack all their possessions. Fire hit Lake? How likely was that? The prevailing winds were from the southwest, and fire couldn't possibly travel across the broad expanse of the lake. Nevertheless, I copied all my computer files and took the copies to storage in Atlantic City, Wyoming.

Listening to the park radio traffic, it seemed clear the backcountry had a lower priority than the front country. The radio chatter included occasional requests from people fighting their own lonely skirmishes. A woman's voice calmly recited her supply list: "twenty-inch Stihl chains, another chain saw, and if possible, some milk and fresh fruit. Is anyone else going to come in here?" she asked. The reply was curt, "No." I wondered how long she had been on the front line. I heard Ranger Ann Marie Chytra call for a bucket drop at Heart Lake Patrol Cabin, eight miles from the nearest road and surrounded on three sides by forest. But the fire manager flying over on reconnaissance had other priorities and would have refused the request. District Ranger Jerry Mernin at the Snake River Station cut in to ask Ann Marie what she really needed. "I need a bucket drop," she said; a wall of fire was approaching, and all they had to defend the cabin were fire pumps and buckets. After hearing this dialog, the fire manager reconsidered. Ranger Chytra got her bucket drop and saved the cabin.

Terry experienced firsthand the danger caused by the lack of resources in the backcountry. He and Lester took the park's boat across the lake to evacuate supplies, including some of the Phillips family's saddles and tack from the Trail Creek barn about twenty miles across the lake. Fires were the last thing on their minds; they were too busy worrying about the poorly designed barge they pulled behind the boat. Part of an old Army pontoon bridge, the barge was built like a giant, iron tea cup with its sides extending only eighteen inches above the water—clearly not designed for travel in three to six-foot waves that regularly whip Yellowstone Lake. Knowing the barge would fill in such waves, Terry and Lester figured their only hope when they reached Trail Creek was to fill the barge quickly and get back home before the winds picked up.

As Terry and Lester approached the cabin, they saw flames just a quarter mile from it, fire hoses on the dock, but no firefighters anywhere in sight. Apparently they had been assigned to another, more urgent site. Lester radioed to Lake for help, but they knew it would take three or four hours before a crew could be mustered and transported across the lake. So Terry and Lester primed the pumps and started wetting down the cabin area. By the time the fire crew relieved them and they had loaded the barge, white caps dotted the lake. As they motored from the southeast arm into the open lake, the winds picked up and the barge took on water, dropping lower and lower into the lake. It would not go down alone. It would drag the boat—and its passengers—hundreds of feet down to the lake bottom. While Lester focused on steering the boat into the waves, Terry grabbed his knife and desperately sawed at the thick rope holding the sinking barge. Finally, the remaining five rope strands twanged free, and the barge and its cargo descended into the depths. Thanks to quick wits and a sharp knife, the lake was denied two victims.

After returning safely and filling out all the reports, the men hugged their relieved wives and shared their regrets about the loss of the Phillips' saddles. Now they had their own fire adventure to share with the firefighters.

The next day, our neighbor Lorie called and gave us more stories. She had some time off but she was not allowed to come home. She and other firefighters were being herded around Cody as they shopped and ate. The crew had worked 200 hours in the last two weeks, and apparently the fire bosses feared some members would desert. Lorie asked, could we take some fresh clothes to her at the Absaroka Mountain Lodge outside the park? When we ate dinner with the firefighters at the lodge, they reported conditions unlike any they had ever seen. Bob Mahn, who had been fighting fires for almost twenty years, said he watched a single spark hit a big tree and immediately start it on fire. Within minutes, the whole tree torched. Firefighters dug firebreaks with their pulaskis (a combination axe and hoe) until they felt their backs would break, but they wondered if they were doing any good. If the winds could blow sparks across highways and even across the Grand Canyon of the Yellowstone, why bother? The Clover Fire had expanded from 300 acres to more than 4,000 acres in just a few hours. How could a few hundred pulaskis control that?

Several Lake-area maintenance workers were fighting fires. One night near the fire line, Art Truman couldn't sleep so he counted trees crashing down—twenty in forty-five minutes. The crackling of the burning trees reminded another of our neighbors, Lowell Baltz, of 1,000 pounds of bacon frying on a hot griddle. Lowell watched a wall of flame consume a grove of spruce trees: half an acre of 24"-diameter trees, gone in a flash. "The smoke was so thick sometimes you had to chew it before you inhaled it," he said. The firefighters came to dread cloudless days. The morning sky turned a sickly grayish yellow, and the afternoon breezes kicked up the flames again. Sleeping in a soggy safe area one night, Lowell heard hooves galloping by. Elk or moose, he figured. Although fire work was difficult, the pay was good. Lorie made $3,500 in two weeks. She said if we had to evacuate, grab her photo albums and her cat. One firefighter told us people in Cody looked disdainfully at them, questioning why they had not put out the fires. He asked me, "Do you know any journalists? Could you tell them we're trying really hard?" People in Jackson, Wyoming, at least appreciated that the folks on the ground with their pulaskis weren't making policy. They put signs all over town saying, "Firefighters, Jackson loves you!"

As we drove home after dinner that day, Terry and I stopped at a pullout above the lake to watch the Clover Mist Fire. While we stared at the flames and replayed the firefighters' stories, my delusions about our safety faded. The next day we heard the news: Our escape route to the east over Sylvan Pass would probably be closed, and the Old Faithful Fire simultaneously would head northeast to Lake. The visitors kept coming. Some were horrified and blamed the flames on park policies. One angrily told me the park's "real" philosophy: "Let the animals starve; let the forests all burn; and let the worms eat the fish."

I wasn't sure what to think. We sat up talking about fire with the naturalists who lived at Lake, and we read everything we could. A century of fire suppression had contributed to the problems. Earlier land managers—the American Indians—had utilized fire to keep grasslands and forests healthy. Elk and other creatures needed meadows, not dense forests, to thrive. The lodgepole pine had evolved to depend on fire to propagate; many lodgepoles needed intense heat to melt their cones' waxy coating and release their seeds. Without fire, they didn't release. Our neighbor Guida Veronda (a long-time park ranger-naturalist) told me to try it myself. Sure enough, a cone that I set on the dashboard opened after a few hours of heat. When the U.S. Army had arrived to manage the park in 1886, they had brought the fire suppression philosophy now personified by Smokey Bear. In our hikes around the park, we had seen many areas almost impassable because of dead, fallen trees, just waiting for a fire.

I saw plenty of questionable decisions by park fire managers that year, which wasn't surprising considering they often had to make split-second choices with unpredictable results. Initially I, too, blamed the park for not responding fast enough to the extraordinary weather conditions. But after talking with firefighters, I became convinced humans could not control nature this time, with her full power unleashed. Mother Nature was still boss, no matter how much money, technology, and manpower the park threw at the fires. That lack of control was difficult for many people to grasp. One visitor said the park should acquire three B-52s for such occasions: "Bomb the hell out of it, just like we did Vietnam." I didn't blame the visitors for being angry. President Reagan had appeared on television to advise tourists the park was still open. Wyoming Governor Mike Sullivan sent out hundreds of personal letters inviting people to visit Yellowstone and telling them they would experience "little or no inconvenience" from the fires. When the visitors arrived, some found themselves stranded hundreds of miles from their campsites when fires burned across the roads, or trapped for hours with roads closed both behind and in front of them.

Ranger Jerry Mernin was infuriated when the park public affairs office in Mammoth actually asked him to predict times when he expected the South Entrance to close. For weeks, his staff had been trying to soothe the nerves of distraught visitors, stiff with fear. At one point, he led a procession of twenty cars and motor homes, inching their way through smoke so thick they could see only one car-length ahead. Suddenly flames flared toward them, but Mernin knew he couldn't ask the drivers to turn around; motor homes can't turn around on the narrow park roads. Somehow, they managed to travel beyond the flames. If one person had had a heart attack from the smoke, or a flat tire, or even had stopped suddenly, the situation could have ended in tragedy, Mernin said. Every morning the rangers awakened wondering whether Yellowstone would suffer an air collision. Without an air control tower, park rangers and fire managers had to juggle more than fifty helicopters and eighteen planes, including World War II bombers, transporting firefighters and dropping fire retardant.

On August 19, Scott and Sheri—Terry's kids—escaped, snaking out between road closures. Cindy's paper plate, darkened and smoking ominously, suddenly burst into flame on August 20—Black Saturday.

That day, 55-mile-an-hour winds fanned the Red–Shoshone Fire back into the Grant area for the second time and forced an immediate evacuation. Wind gusts reached eighty miles an hour. Meanwhile, a new fire roared like a locomotive toward Flagg Ranch on the park's south boundary, forcing evacuation of that tourist center. Directly in that fire's path after Flagg Ranch was the ranger station—home to the Mernins and another ranger's family. Many tourists were trapped on the road between the two fires. The park radio chattered frantically as park officials closed roads leading into those fires.

From the lakeshore, Terry and I watched the forested ridge above West Thumb crown out in flames. Black columns of smoke rolled out over the water, whipped by wind into six-foot waves. That dramatic sight burned through our denial. The whole park could torch. On Black Saturday, 165,000 acres burned. We started to develop two contingency plans—one plan if we had a day's warning, another for an hour's warning. I gathered our important papers and started lists of what else to take—dogs, family history scroll, photo albums, sleeping bags, address books, and computer. Later I saw that my husband had added: "Terry." I wouldn't forget to evacuate him!

I expected Alice Siebecker and her partner, Brian Crandell, to scorn our efforts. He was a professional fireman, teaching firefighter classes all over Montana. However, they shared our grave concern and had set their own evacuation priorities: 1) guns, 2) computer, 3) cat, according to Brian. Cat, computer, and guns, according to Alice. Lois Lounsbury had been a firefighter early in her career so she kept the park radio off and focused on her work at the hospital. After I shared our plans with her, she started thinking about her grandmother's diamond ring and the horses. Terry—Mr. Cool—didn't seem to worry. He just prepared, filling the gas tanks and airing the tires on our vehicles, and putting gasoline, propane, food, and sleeping bags in the houseboat so we could evacuate by water.

I went to the ranger station to get another fire map, which were issued daily to show the various fires' progress. There, I overheard distraught visitors saying, "Our AAA Trip Plans showed exactly which roads to take, but those roads are on fire. What should we do?" One visitor had left his heart medicine at the campground in Grant, and he couldn't get back. Does he really have to drive hundreds of miles roundabout through Wyoming to retrieve it? Yes, he was told, he does. The rangers tried to deal with each question patiently, but their thoughts focused on friends in the backcountry whose lives were on the line. In mid-August, two backcountry rangers had called for a helicopter to pull them out of Howell Creek. White smoke had turned black, and the fire was making a run at them. But no helicopter could respond—one was down for repair, another for maintenance. Retreating to the creek, the men spent two terrifying hours lying in the shallow water under their fire shelters while the fire roared over the creek. They survived.

On August 25, we heard Dave Phillips's voice on the radio, and something caught my attention. We often heard voices shake a little on the radio during those anxious days, but Dave was known for his cool head. He calmly described where he and Kathleen were located. His next words conveyed a different mes-

beyond their coyote camp.

A few days later, on August 23, they heard an incredible roar, like a 707 jet trying to take off, and they saw a wall of flames a quarter mile long lunging toward them. Finally at about 11 P.M., the fire lay down for the night, as wildfires do in the cooler hours. For some time, the Phillips had been planning to leave Yellowstone the following day and return home to California. Their replacements—Rangers Wes Miles and Dan Ehlen—already had arrived to take over. Dave and Kathleen fell into a fitful sleep, knowing the respite would be temporary and that their trip out of the Thorofare would not be easy. They also found it difficult to abandon their post on the eve of battle, after planning for weeks on how to protect the ranger station, but it was too late to change their minds.

The next day, as Dave instructed Wes and Dan, Kathleen saddled their horses and loaded the pack animals, talking soothingly to them. At best, they faced a couple of long days. Their normal, thirty-two-mile route (north along the east bank of the Yellowstone River and the eastern shore of Yellowstone Lake) was out of the question. With deep grass on fire and many burned trees downed, it would be too difficult for the horses. As far as they could tell, every drainage leading out of the Thorofare had either burned or was on fire. They settled upon Falcon Creek, knowing it would require a strenuous, 1,400 feet climb to Two Ocean Plateau and down the other side. Falcon Creek, too, had partially burned. Warned before their departure about fire ahead, they abandoned the trail part way up and bushwhacked the rest of the way up and over Two Ocean Plateau. To avoid falling trees, they watched for trees burned through at the bottom. Each time they entered a burned area and trees fell with a crackling thud nearby, the horses acted uneasy but, drawing confidence from their human companions, they didn't panic. With so many steep cliffs between them and their destination, it took time to find a route down. They arrived at the Fox Creek cabin nine hours later, having traveled only about twenty-four miles on their circuitous route.

The next day they traveled down the Snake River drainage toward their destination—Heart Lake. Up until that point, the trip had been uneventful for two people seasoned by weeks of fire—only a few columns of smoke, some fairly close but no immediate danger. As they approached Heart Lake, however, they discovered the fire there had blown up that day. Continuing along the trail, they rode through areas of ground fire and heavy, choking smoke, interspersed with green areas. They never knew when the flames close to the ground might take off into the tree crowns and become a roaring conflagration. Finally the smoke got so thick they could not see what lay ahead. Were they about to enter an impassable inferno? There was only one way to find out. Dave got off his horse, tied it, and walked ahead. Kathleen watched as he disappeared into the smoke. Before he went, he reported his location on the radio: Dante's Inferno.

Kathleen sat waiting, alone with the horses, her thoughts a jumble. The four horses and one mule stood dead still, fully alert but not moving a muscle. As she waited, green patches of thought emerged through the smoke in her head. If the torching trees came right at her, she had to figure out how to get out of there. Should she backtrack or go forward? Even as her personal survival instincts kicked in, she thought about the horses, vowing to untie the others before she took off on her horse to find a safe spot.

Finally Dave reemerged and said they could go forward. He led the mule, and the horses followed. Riding at the rear, Kathleen could barely make out the horse in front of her, much less Dave. Trees crashed to the ground; fire roared on three sides of their path. Kathleen said a quick prayer that they could get through the path ahead, while she tried to keep her cool. After a few interminable minutes, they escaped the most serious fires and made their way to the Heart Lake cabin. Their clothing and their horses were coated with thick soot, but they were alive. Ranger Ann Marie Chytra enthusiastically welcomed them to her post, and Dave and Kathleen collapsed inside. Later, munching on fresh-baked pizza, they laughed giddily as they traded stories, knowing how close they had come to never seeing one another again. While Ann Marie had always considered herself an adrenalin junkie, the fires cured her.

Dave and Kathleen arrived at Lake just in time for the annual cheesecake contest. Although some had argued the contest should be skipped, others said they needed it to help relieve the relentless anxiety. While several had stories of close escapes, none were as dramatic as the Phillips'.

Mary Taber stole the stage at the cheesecake contest when she quietly mentioned that she had spent the most romantic weekend of her life at the Trail Creek cabin. The room turned quiet as heads turned toward Mary, a slender woman known for her outdoor skills, her ability to intimidate lawbreakers with a single look, and her storytelling. In the front country, she supervised the night shift of rangers who handled drunken employees and grizzlies in the campgrounds. During the fires, however, she took several assignments in the backcountry.

She had planned to spend just a couple of days at Trail Creek, but the fires constantly changed everyone's plans. Mary had to relay her regrets to a certain helicopter pilot over the park radio, knowing that half the park was listening. Curt and Mary had been trying to get together for a date for several weeks, but each time, fires interfered. The next day she heard the unmistakable whir of helicopter blades. Everyone knew there was no place to land a helicopter at the Trail Creek cabin on the shore of Yellowstone Lake, but Curt was known for his daring work rescuing firefighters during the fires. Sure enough, it was Curt. When he lowered one skid onto the boat dock, hovering his helicopter half over the water, Mary ran out to see what was wrong. He handed her a single, red rose before he lifted off and disappeared down the lakeshore.

Most of the conversation at the cheesecake party sounded like a therapy session as everyone sorted out their emotions about the long summer of fires. Many had seen a favorite trail or a favorite campsite turn black. But Kathleen talked about the Lynx Creek area that had burned earlier. There amongst the burned trees, new blades of grass were coming up, and a lupine had blossomed. The purple flowers promised renewal.

After the party, there was little time for nostalgia or story telling. Tension rose as the fires came closer to Lake. By September, many of the seasonals like Kathleen and Dave had left the park, and several others were gone fighting fires in other parts of the park. By September 5, more than 9,600 people were fighting fires in Yellowstone. Terry and the remaining maintenance crew were working twelve-hour days. While I worked I tried to ignore the increased level of activity in our backyard, turning Pavorotti music up full blast to drown out the whine of chainsaws, and the splatter of hoses wetting down the backyard. The booming tenor helped, and I actually got a few pages of rewriting done. The roads to the north, west, and east were closed: The rangers put duct tape over all destinations on the sign at Fishing Bridge junction.

I didn't like being threatened at the same time as Old Faithful and Mammoth; I knew they would get priority. We had one fire truck—our regular year-around tanker truck—and five trained firefighters to cover the whole Lake/Fishing Bridge area. Almost all of our firefighters, hoses, nozzles, hose connections, spanner wrenches, and hydrant wrenches had been shanghaied by other areas. We knew there were more people living at the other locations than Lake, but couldn't they leave us even a couple of fire trucks?

Ranger Mary Taber lived in the dumpy, old Mission 66 houses built as temporary structures in the 1950s. Fire officials told her they would not even try to save those structures. They said, "If the fire gets within a mile, we're going to torch it, and say wildfire took it out—maybe then region will pay for new housing." She wasn't sure if they were kidding, and everything she owned was at risk.

Our multiplex was good enough to be defended, but after the North Fork Fire hit Old Faithful on September 7, Terry began to wonder whether there was anything that could protect the housing at Lake. At Old Faithful, tornado-like winds created by the advancing fire tossed fist-sized embers and bent full-sized trees. Gases preceding the fire burst suddenly into flame, destroying everything in their path, including seventeen buildings. The foam and sprinkler systems could not have protected the park's most famous structure, the Old Faithful Inn. Only a slight shift in the wind direction saved it. As the Old Faithful employees were being evacuated, they met visitors coming in to watch the geyser. Visitors were still wandering around, asking directions, when the firestorm hit. On September 8, President Reagan sent Interior Secretary Donald Hodel, Agriculture Secretary Richard Lyng, and Undersecretary of Defense William Taft to Yellowstone on a fact-finding mission. They promised more help from the military and a review of fire management policy. On September 10, Yellowstone was closed to the public for the first time in history.

Yellowstone Lake was the only barrier anywhere in the park that had stopped the advancing flames—so far. But the fires weren't done. After hitting Old Faithful, the North Fork Fire stretched a menacing finger into a six-mile front, just northwest of us. Ranger Alice Siebecker called on September 9 to ask if I would join the fuel reduction team, moving firewood, chopping off lower limbs, and hauling potential fuel out of the area, and I eagerly agreed. The morning report predicted winds out of the northwest with gusts of forty miles per hour, which we knew could deliver fire to our doorstep. They were evacuating all "non-essential" personnel from Lake and Mammoth, but if I were working, I would become essential and maybe they wouldn't make me leave. I couldn't stand the thought of abandoning my husband, my friends, and my home. After all the months of waiting, I wanted to see what happened.

I stopped drinking my morning tea while listening to NPR news each morning. I didn't need caffeine with all the adrenalin. Broadcasters reported a group called "The Light Connection" had called for a nationwide meditation and prayer at 8 P.M. Saturday to bring rain to Yellowstone. They called it the "Yellowstone Instant of Cooperation." The weatherman breezily predicted the winds might be disastrous for Yellowstone, but they would be delightful for the America Cup races off the coast at San Diego. We fire laborers focused on protecting the power lines, as well as the dwellings. If we lost power, we couldn't pump water into the reservoirs, which fed the fire hydrants. With the fire hydrants going full blast, the reservoirs would be drained in four hours. A busload of Army guys showed up, their enthusiasm fired by their youth and fraternity. They whooped with delight when they saw the giant logs, waiting for conquest. They threw them into the waiting trucks to be hauled away.

Back in the housing area, Chris Lilley hauled her valuables to her car—two giant bags of stuffed animals and her photo albums. Mark Marschall and Kathi Noaker packed their mountain bikes, several pairs of skis, climbing ropes, and carabiners. Lois Lounsbury was most worried about her grandmother's diamond ring and the horses. All the roads leading out of Lake were closed. We knew our local roads could soon become impassable with fallen trees. Terry figured he could run the giant Walters V-plow three miles to the marina at Bridge Bay, pushing burning logs out of the way if necessary. From Bridge Bay, we would take the houseboat onto the lake. Watching our neighbors' choices about "valuables," I prayed we wouldn't have to make choices about which five neighbors would fit on the houseboat.

After work, I drove to Bridge Bay to hose down the houseboat so it would be less likely to catch fire from flying embers. I stood on the boat's roof watching the awful glow from the North Fork Fire to the northwest. The red sun flashed occasionally from behind the giant cumulus cloud, which undulated wildly in the wind. The blood-red water quivered in the nearly empty marina. To the east, the sky above the Clover Mist Fire looked heavy and purplish-grey, like the sky before a tornado. What would the morning bring?

On September 11, we looked outside and saw a few white ashes drifting toward the ground. But it wasn't ashes; it was snow! We called each other excitedly to share the jubilant news. We're safe! We don't have to evacuate! Local radio stations played "Jingle Bells." Within hours, the danger was over. One-quarter inch of precipitation had accomplished what millions of dollars and thousands of people could not. The snow put out the fires. By then, nearly 800,000 acres had burned inside the park, approximately thirty-six percent of the park's area. The fires shattered illusions about the power of man and machines. We were reminded once again: Mother Nature writes the rules.

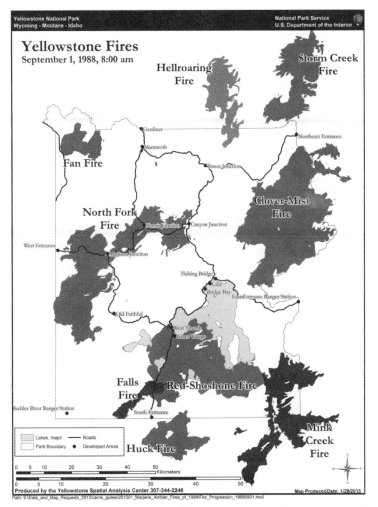

On September 1, 1988, nine fires still raged in or near Yellowstone National Park. By September 5, more than 9,600 people were fighting the fires in the park, but the only thing that stopped the fires was snow that fell on September 11. (Map produced by the Yellowstone Spatial Analysis Center)

CHAPTER SIXTEEN
Ladies Aid Society

Blessed are the flexible, for they shall not be bent out of shape.
—GWYNNE SPENCER

*F*OR THE FIRST FEW YEARS WE LIVED AT LAKE, WOMEN
of the park's interior congregated once each winter for
lunch. In the outside world, this wouldn't demand much com-
mitment. Just rearrange the work schedule, call the babysitter,
and go. For us, it was different. Depending upon where we lived,
we had to snowmobile twenty to fifty miles—without our husbands along to break trail or fix the snowmachines. Ladies Aid
Societies during the Civil War provided supplies to soldiers and
cared for the sick and wounded soldiers; later these organizations
quilted together and fought for woman suffrage. Our gatherings
offered support for one another in the sometimes hostile land
where we lived. Could Yellowstone accommodate women and
families? Could we prove up and earn our stake there? It still was
not clear to me.

In January, we had planned to meet for lunch at Grant, but
when I awoke on the appointed day and listened to the wind
whistling through the door jam, I pictured horrible road condi-

tions along the lakeshore between Lake and Grant. I knew from experience a wind like that blowing across the lake would form drifts perpendicular to the road; the road workers called them "finger drifts," probably because they were spaced so closely together. Some days they were six feet high, and challenged even the best snowmobilers. Then they looked more like shoulder drifts to me.

Should we go? Remembering Lois Lounsbury's and my surprisingly euphoric enthusiasm as we made plans, the answer would be yes—as long as Lorie would help us start our snow machines and break trail. Both Lois and I were more comfortable on skis, and we occasionally needed someone's help starting our aged machines. Mary McCutcheon called from Canyon to say she was still coming. But what about Cindy Mernin? Could she make it twenty-two miles from the Snake River Ranger Station at the South Entrance, to Grant? They received eighteen inches of snow Friday night and twelve inches Saturday, so she would be bucking thirty inches of powder.

Sure enough, Lorie had to pull start my old Ski-doo snowmachine after I flooded it. Starting the machines was much more intimidating than riding them. The temperature was warm—about 30 degrees—and I gave it too much prime. I knew what to do to dry it out, but I was just not strong enough to pull the rope with one hand several times while holding the throttle with the other. Those two-cycle engines can drive a person mad, like the chainsaw I fought each fall at Atlantic City, Wyoming. When our little wagon train headed out toward Grant, the road stretched untracked before us. Terry had taken the DMC groomer east to clear the drifts and avalanche debris from Sylvan Pass; he wouldn't be grooming this road until the following day. No snowmobile traffic had reached that far into the park yet.

Lorie took the lead and punched through the drifts. She never ridiculed a woman for timidity. She remembered her own first

year in the park interior too well. Although the drifts reached a
foot above the road, they weren't as big as I had feared, and by
then I actually enjoyed snowmobiling. I learned to do Jane Fonda
exercises for a month before snowmobiling season to get my neck
and arms ready, and sometimes I crouched above the seat to let my
knees rather than my back absorb the jolts. Traveling in a caravan
of four, I could relish how wintry the frozen lake looked without
worrying. In August we would have risked our lives to stand in the
middle of the highway here. But when we stopped and turned off
our machines at Pumice Point to look for otters on the lake ice, all
we could hear was the wind and the "widowmakers." That term
must have come from lumber camps where falling trees would kill
the loggers. In Yellowstone, the fifty-foot-high lodgepole pines
whined as they swayed, snow boiling off the branches in whirling
swirls. At least six people have died in Yellowstone from falling
trees, according to park historian Lee Whittlesey, but even I could
not worry about that happening as we whizzed by.

When we arrived at Grant, we heard all about Cindy's challenges. Because the snow was so deep, her machine didn't have
enough power to start forward with her on the seat. Instead, she
grabbed the throttle, half ran alongside, and was half dragged by
the machine until it had sufficient momentum for her to clamber
on, much like dogsled racers in Alaska. For the entire twenty-two
miles she could barely see through her face shield, filled with snow
from her traumatic start. She didn't dare stop; she was sure her
machine couldn't push the snow from a dead stop again. When
she arrived, she described her trip to us with great relish. "Almost
like the old days," she exclaimed. "Paradise isn't for sissies!"

At Grant, the maintenance crew had created a tropical beach
of sorts around a hot tub. After piling our snowmobile suits
among the palm tree posters and lawn chairs, we joined the other
women and pulled out our sack lunches and our collection of
stories. It always felt so festive when we gathered. As much as we

enjoyed our own tiny communities, we needed fresh infusions of stories and perspectives.

The first topic was a letter sent recently to the chief ranger, expressing outrage that the park would provide winter employees with a hot tub in each district and that a rich Texan was considering contributing satellite dishes. The critic said, "If YNP's employees are bored silly, the situation should be corrected not by turning employee quarters into health spas and television caves, but by hiring people who would rather go skiing by moonlight than lounge on their duffs watching the Saturday night videos." What a purist, we muttered. What does he suggest we do on the twenty nights per month without moonlight? What about the people who aren't strong enough to ski? And the mothers who don't have a babysitter within fifty miles? Where does he suggest the park service go to find fifteen clones of himself to fill the jobs of water utility foreman, groomer, wife, ranger, and roof shoveler? Let him walk a mile in our Pacs (insulated boots) before he smarts off!

When the park circulated the questionnaire asking what we wanted in our districts, Terry and I had requested a piano in a common area at Lake. We enjoyed community storytelling more than television and dreamed that maybe we could have community music making. However, we understood that people who had to snowmobile hundreds of miles a week would appreciate a hot tub to warm up and sooth their aching joints.

Someone else told our group about a letter to the Billings Gazette called "Give Park Back to Nature," which criticized the park for spending so much money to upgrade employee housing. He said all permanent park employee housing should be moved into gateway communities outside the park. Apparently the writer had little understanding of the size of the park: Gateway communities were located hours away from many locations. If the rangers had to commute an hour and a half out of the park each evening in the winter, who would handle snowmobile accidents or visitor medical emergencies? During the summer, who would drive thirty to fifty miles to respond to nighttime gunfights in the campgrounds over firewood, or drunk drivers, or bears in the campgrounds? Who would get out the front-end loader at 3 A.M. to move a dead bison off the road? This park is big.

We were surprised and pleased that park administrators were actually concerned about employee housing and the quality of life in the park interior. It had taken decades to improve living conditions. Cindy had to fight just to get the shutters off her windows and a record player to break the silence. Scotty and Louise Chapmans' home/ranger station burned down because of its primitive refrigerator. Alice and Bob Murphy had to buy someone else's choice of food to get them through the long winter. Why did living in Yellowstone have to be so difficult? Did they figure the glamour would sustain us? Had the park service conspired against women and families, or were their experiences just inevitable on the frontier?

In her book *National Parks and the Woman's Voice: A History*, historian Polly Welts Kaufman provided a national perspective for our questions and explained what shaped the park service policies through the years. Kaufman interviewed 43 wives and a total of 343 women across the country. She also utilized 560 questionnaires from park service women, and freelance journalist Dorothy Boyle Huyck's recorded interviews of park service women.

She documents women's efforts since the turn of the twentieth century to "domesticate the national parks." It was not easy because of the national parks' "militaristic chivalrous culture and all-male tradition." The Yellowstone area was utilized by many different Native American tribes (including men, women and children) for centuries, most recently by Sheepeater Indians, but when non-Indian mountain men and poachers arrived, they did not bring their families. After Congress created Yellowstone National Park in 1872, it soon realized the park would have to be protected from poachers and from tourists throwing soap into geyser pools and hauling off invaluable resources. In 1886, the U.S. Army was sent to protect the park. So three decades of military administration preceded the creation of the National Park Service in 1916. These military roots—and the focus on protection—continued to haunt park service employees and families for decades.

For example, enlisted men's wives were not allowed to live in the park (although officers' wives were). This all-male tradition continued after the National Park Service took over, and only single men were hired as park rangers at first. Later the park lifted the ban on hiring married men, but in the early years the rangers who were stationed at backcountry stations were expected to live apart from their families. The park service used the poor condition of the ranger stations/homes as an argument for not allowing wives to live there and, later, for not hiring women as employees. "They [ranger stations] were not adequate for anyone but those of pioneer spirit," one of the wives interviewed by Kaufman said. However, young rangers objected to the policy and demanded that their wives be allowed to join them in the park. Married in 1932, Scotty and Louise Chapman apparently were among the first two couples that the park service allowed to live together in Yellowstone's backcountry.

The Chapmans, Murphys, and Mernins were lucky compared with other families in southwestern United States parks, who lived in tents among the scorpions, centipedes, and rattlesnakes. Being isolated was preferable to the wives who complained about having to have their houses clean and the dishes washed before the first visitors arrived at their visitor centers/homes. As early as the 1930s, Yellowstone wives raised concerns about substandard housing that threatened the future of the National Park Service because of unhappiness and turnover, according to Kaufman. In

1952, park service wives led an effort to improve housing, and their report was submitted to Congress. They found that three-fourths of the qualified applicants were married, but they could not be considered because of the lack of housing. Seasonal employees were still housed in tents, even in Yellowstone where snow can fall any month of the year. As a result of the wives' efforts, the park service put considerable resources into improving housing nationwide as part of Mission 66 (a ten-year program for capital improvements to be completed by the service's fiftieth anniversary in 1966).

We Yellowstone wives in the 1980s and 1990s prided ourselves on our pioneering spirit. We often pitched in to help our spouses at their work, without compensation, and tried not to grumble about the lack of regular mail service or email. Kathleen O'Leary accepted the lack of power and running water at Thorofare Ranger Station where her husband, Dave Phillips, was assigned, and she cheerfully took on a big share of the work. We knew families at some national parks were even more isolated: At Guadalupe Mountain National Park in Texas, the nearest convenience store for the two residents was an eighty-minute drive away; in Utah at Canyonlands National Park's Maze District, the ranger's family was six hours' drive from the nearest town, and there were no schools, no mail service, and no employment for spouses.

Nevertheless, it was difficult to deal with the cavalier attitudes of Yellowstone administrators who did not appreciate our sacrifices. The Mission 66 standardized approach to housing created problems of its own. I tried to console the wife of a permanent employee who was weeping after being insulted by a park official. She had dared to complain about her uninsulated house, where condensation rained down on her carpet and personal book collection. Although housing for permanent employees dramatically improved while we were there in the 1990s, seasonal employees still lived in temporary portable housing erected forty years earlier, and the furnaces had been condemned.

As we traded stories at our ladies' lunch at Grant, we learned that a park official had told employees concerned about summer child-care in the park interior: "If you aren't happy, you should look for work elsewhere." Despite the growing number of women rangers and maintenance workers, families still were expected to adapt to men's terms. Housing and child-care were not the only problems for wives who followed their husbands from park to park. I was lucky. I was able to pursue my writing career while living in the park. Cindy Mernin was not the only wife who had to choose between her husband and her career. A book written many years earlier, *Never Marry a Ranger*, took a light-hearted approach to the subject, and women rangers gave copies to male spouses as a joke. But to many wives, marrying a park service employee meant giving up their own career dreams. Kaufman said, "Some wives lost their entire sense of self....Her destiny was to be lived out through her husband, the parks, and their children." One woman told Kaufman, "My self esteem was bruised because I was so dependent upon my husband's income. I wanted a partnership, not a dependency."

Lois Lounsbury served as the administrator for Lake Hospital during the summer and as the liaison for park medical issues. She told our gathering at Grant that somebody at headquarters had called her the week before and said the park wanted to hire a psychologist to counsel people in the interior since "we all drink too much." As she told the story, someone said petulantly, "Mammoth people have a lot more psychological problems than we have!" Besides, if we had psychological problems, would we be willing to snowmobile to Mammoth to see the psychologist? That would just cause more stress.

As I had grown to expect, we also talked snowmobile over lunch. At one of our lunches a woman from park headquarters had asked in wonder, "Do you talk about snowmobiles all the time here?" No, just in the fall when we're feeling anxious about the arrival of the season. And in the winter when it dominates our lives. And in the spring, when we're liberated from it. When it came to snowmobiling, we found we had more in common with each other than with our own husbands. We're caught between drives forged by the feminism of the 1980s and those of a much earlier era. We slid too easily into "his work" (the cars and the snowmachines and getting in and out of the park) and "her" work (the meals and the house). Snowmobiling brought out the Cinderella Complex in many of us: It was always "his" fault when something went wrong.

Ranger Colette Daigle, Lorie, Ranger Alice Siebecker, and Cindy were quiet through our curses and complaints. Alice said she probably snowmobiled 6,000 miles per year, just on her government machine, not counting her personal machine. Collette reminded us of her relief to begin snowmobiling after driving on slick roads with wheeled vehicles for a few weeks. She had slid off the narrow, curvy road below Mammoth and nosed over the edge above the Gardner River before her car came to a stop.

The women who snowmobiled for a living accepted snowmobiling as just one of the costs of their careers in the National Park Service. Women had come a long way since the days when Louise Chapman only got paid for her work in Yellowstone when all the men were off to war. When they returned, she and other wives across the country were off the payroll. Lorie Rippley had moved up from Bear Forage Technician and roof shoveler. Through the benefits of the Equal Employment Opportunity program, her dedication, and her boss Hume Lilley's confidence in her, she was being trained as a utility systems operator assistant where she repaired plumbing, helped to operate the sewer lift stations, tested drinking water quality, and dealt with clogged sewer lines. She became accustomed to having sewage splash in her face as a normal part of the job. She was just glad to be working outside and not sitting in an office.

Despite the administrative changes that had made it possible for them to advance, women encountered discrimination and rude behavior when they entered fields formerly reserved for men. Terry and I met Helen Wolfe at Lake when she worked as a cook for the plow crew one year. One of the first women to work for the park's Maintenance Division, she had begun by cleaning the campground at Canyon in 1967. She later worked elsewhere in the park. She told us, "Visitors from back East were resentful. A lot of men would say, 'What did you take a man's job away from him for?'" One boss told her that he didn't want a woman working in his area. Another told obscene jokes every day to humiliate her. She said women often were deliberately given the heaviest, largest tools. "It's true that women have to work three times as hard as men at some things to get anywhere," she said. Twenty years later, Lorie's humor helped her deal with the guys' guff. "If they gave it to me, I gave it back." She realized she could not lift as much as they did, but she still wanted to earn their respect. "I don't spit and cuss like the guys though."

Sometimes the women rangers also felt they had to work three times as hard as the men in other ways. They had to shoot better and know more holds for wrestling prisoners into handcuffs. One of the smaller women rangers, Mary Taber, could make herself eight feet tall when necessary; her persona expanded her personal power and intimidated the would-be offenders. Alice Siebecker made us laugh at our Grant tropical party with her story of rescuing a burly New York City policeman who would rather have frozen than be helped by a "girl ranger." For the most part, however, she said she was treated well her entire career.

Reading Kaufman would have made Lorie and the women rangers at our gathering even more appreciative of their opportunities. Kaufman uncovered a strange period in park service history, unknown to most of the women who now enjoy their jobs so much. Beginning in 1918, the park service began hiring women as ranger-naturalists who gave educational programs, and others who worked as protection rangers, some of whom wore the Stetson, the badge, and the gun and patrolled on horseback. But the women's presence threatened the male image of the ranger so much that in 1926 the park service ordered the park superintendents to stop hiring women. "This discouraged all but the most secure superintendents from hiring women until the 1960s"— more than thirty years, Kaufman says.

The controversy centered on Yellowstone where Superintendent Horace Albright had hired more women than any other park—ten women as rangers or ranger-naturalists beginning in 1920. Women also worked in those positions at some other national parks at that time. An Interior Department inspector was horrified to find women rangers at Yellowstone. He thought that male rangers should be protecting the park. He objected to both male and female ranger-naturalists, whose work he described as "taking visitors to peer at peewee's nests."

Albright, Yellowstone's first superintendent, was ahead of his times. He felt it was just as important for parks to educate the public as to protect the park resources, and he found that women did a better job of education. He said that, with one or two exceptions, "There is not a member of the permanent force at the present time who could give a lecture if he had to—not even if his life depended upon it." In fact, he assigned some men to outlying sections on fire patrol and protection work so they would not have contact with the public at all. Nevertheless, the inspector's arguments prevailed for decades.

The 1970s and 1980s brought a new era. Finally women could be either ranger-naturalists or law enforcement rangers again. I loved my job continuing Horace Albright's vision of educating the public about the value of parks. After starting work for the National Park Service during the fires, I was later hired as a ranger-naturalist at Fishing Bridge Visitor Center. Most of our staff members were women, but there were several men who certainly kept the visitors enthralled, not like the men Horace Albright mentioned. Unlike the law enforcement rangers, our interactions with the people were generally positive. We heard some ignorant questions, such as "When is the next erection?" and we tried to be polite when visitors insisted they had seen an ostrich, a llama, or a mammoth. People came to the visitor center or programs because they wanted to learn. Many were fulfilling a lifelong dream. One man wanted to show his six-year-old son the Upper and Lower Falls and Old Faithful, but the boy was in a wheelchair. "If it's not too far, I suppose I could carry him." He told me, "We've been as far north as you can get in Alaska and down to Mexico this summer. We have seen every major attraction." I smiled, assuming he just liked to travel. "It's better than paying all that money to doctors and hospitals, don't you think? They told me I only had five months to live," he said, chuckling as if he had played a good joke on the fates.

I appreciated the gains made by women that gave me such a great job, but I felt frustrated by the dearth of American Indian employees or people of any color employed at national parks. We had been warned at our ranger naturalist training that the demographics of the nation were changing, and before long, people of color would outnumber us people of no color. If the park service did not hire African Americans, Hispanics, and Indians, they would not feel connected with the park and would be less likely to support the national parks. With the help of a grant from the Wyoming Council for the Humanities, I brought Indian speakers into the park; but if other national park naturalist programs mentioned Indians at all, they usually relied upon missionary translations of Indian legends.

Terry and I had an opportunity to thank Horace Albright

personally for his role in hiring women when we met him in April 1986 at a nursing home in California. At the time, he was a living bridge between the park's birth and our modern era. He told us about the letters he was writing to then Yellowstone Superintendent Robert Barbee with advice on how to run the park. Even though he had also served as the director of the National Park Service, Yellowstone was the highlight of Albright's career. To him, those were the good old days: "I want my old job back," he told us. He died a year later at the age of ninety-seven.

My drifting thoughts were interrupted as everyone began gathering up their snowmobile suits and boots. Aware of the oncoming darkness, we broke up our gaggle at Grant, strengthened by the knowledge that we were not alone. We had a good time, laughing together at snowmobile stories and grumbling about headquarters and critical outsiders who did not understand us. We were lucky compared with women in the Yellowstone's earlier eras; we had each other. Psychologists have proven that a group's cohesion saves the individuals. For some reason, we had it at Lake, but some of the interior communities did not. I felt it was because they didn't have enough women to serve as support troops, smoothing relationships, bringing people together for potlucks, and protesting when headquarters made our lives more difficult than necessary.

We had no problem returning to Lake, and tried to encourage Mary McCutcheon to stay over rather than risk the seventeen-mile trip alone through Hayden Valley with its drifts and bison bedded down in the roads. It was the first time she had made such a trip without her husband, but she was determined. "It's something I have to do." I understood the sentiment. An hour later, I called to make sure she got home okay. "Yes, I'm glad I did it, but I don't really want to do that often." So what's the alternative? Staying home until he can go? I asked myself. The Cinderella Syndrome is an easy trap to fall into, and as time goes by, it gets

Chapter Seventeen
Babies in Paradise

Life is either a tight rope or a feather bed. Give me the tight rope.

—Edith Wharton

January 3, 1993, dawned cold. The mercury wasn't expected to rise above zero Fahrenheit all day. I tried to call Dan and Karen Reinhart at their home in Livingston, Montana, to report the temperature. I was worried: Their daughter, Emma, was only ten weeks old, a tiny, vulnerable infant, and this was her first snowmobile ride into her new home at Lake. Dan was the new Lake District resource management coordinator. They had purchased an old snowmachine to supplement the one provided to Dan by the National Park Service, but Karen had never operated one. While Dan had spent most of the previous winter at Lake, Karen had visited only once, riding double on the park service snowmachine. Karen and I got to know each other during the previous summer when she lived at Lake, and we immediately bonded, recognizing kindred rebel spirits.

Worried even before I saw the temperature that January morning, I had volunteered to haul a sled up to Mammoth for their gear and escort them into the park. My offer stemmed partly from friendship, partly from my own strengthened confidence at snowmobiling, and partly from my growing realization of the special difficulties faced by families with children.

By then even the heart of Yellowstone was civilized or at least half-civilized compared with when Scotty and Louise Chapman raised their son in Yellowstone. We had relatively reliable snowmobiles and radios, electricity, telephones, and mail service. Nevertheless, children were still exposed to the elements and to the possibilities of accidents. While hoping for their children to be as comfortable in the out of doors as the Chapmans' son, Bill, had been, modern Yellowstone parents worried about their flying off the snowmobiles or losing their hearing from the constant roar. Considering the isolation, a surprising number of children were being raised at different locations in the park, because employees who were a suitable age for the lifestyle were also of childbearing age. The lucky parents who lived at Old Faithful or somewhere else along the main snowcoach routes could transport their small children safe and warm in an enclosed cab. Snowmobiling was the only option for getting to our community.

Karen and Dan had no doubt received plenty of advice. If they had to snowmobile, Yellowstone parents usually would put an infant in an oversized snowsuit with the mom. As they grew older, the options changed. Some harnessed the toddler to the parent so the child wouldn't go flying off the machine. If there were an accident, however, couldn't the child be crushed by the parent landing on top of her? Ugh. The things that parents had to think about. One couple put their toddler in a little sleeping bag, large enough at the bottom so she could straddle the snowmobile. How could they possibly hold securely to a baby while operating a snowmobile? I could barely spare one hand from the handlebars long enough to adjust my helmet. Another couple rode together on one machine—with two children squeezed in between them. How could they manage that?

At least Karen didn't have to snowmobile back and forth when she was pregnant, as other mothers did; their doctors never liked hearing about that. Even worse, a woman we knew suffered a miscarriage in the park interior and then had to snowmobile out to see her doctor.

Normal maladies could quickly become serious in remote areas of the park. Knowing that we depended completely upon each other in a medical emergency, most of the residents at Lake took basic CPR (cardio pulmonary resuscitation) classes, paying special attention to how to conduct CPR on infants and children. We swore we wouldn't go out if the conditions were really bad, but circumstances often overruled good sense. When our neighbor Mona Divine's cat got sick, it was -20° F so she bundled plastic bottles filled with hot water around her cat in a wooden box. You couldn't do that with a child. The previous Lake resource management coordinator and our next-door neighbors, Roger Andrascik and his wife Karen, had moved to another park and, soon after, their two-and-a-half-year-old son came down with bronchiolitis, a life-threatening illness that requires immediate hospitalization. Fortunately, they were able to get Sean to the hospital in time. If it had happened at Lake during the winter, he probably would not have made it in time.

We didn't know how much to tell Karen and Dan about such stories. Our rangers had training as EMTs, but would that be enough for a serious problem? Sometimes helicopters were available, but often they were not. Parents had few choices. If they did not want to home school or expose their children to the hazards of snowmobiling, some mothers chose to stay outside of the park, separated from their husbands all week. Other wives wanted to pursue their own careers rather than sitting at home like frontier wives: cooking, cleaning, and going stir crazy. It was the 1980s after all.

Most of us appreciated the beauty of Yellowstone in winter.

As Dan Reinhart said, "No bugs, no bears, and no people." But it was not an easy place to live. News that the Carter family applied for a hardship transfer had rumbled through the interior community like an earthquake. We knew they had a couple of rough trips out for groceries with their baby, but leave Yellowstone? After paying the price of living in one of the interior park communities for only four months (December-April), they had rejected the reward—summer. Several interior women reacted with guilt to the news. If only we hadn't told so many bear stories at Stacy Carter's welcoming party... If only we had offered to babysit more... But most of us lived at least twenty miles away, and some would have had to snowmobile with their own babies to get there.

The Carters' decision set us to buzzing over what our life was really about. We generally accepted the hardships, muttering about how headquarters didn't appreciate what we went through, but very deliberately not dwelling on the negatives. We did not consider the Exit Option, at least not until someone decided to leave so abruptly. By then Lorie Rippley had resigned and moved outside the park. When I called her in Havre, Montana, and told her about the Carters' decision, she had no trouble understanding. Yellowstone winters were tough enough even without children. After eight winters in Yellowstone, she had just spent her first winter on the outside and tasted liberation. She couldn't imagine spending another winter as a single person imprisoned by snow. Maybe if she were married. But why would she want to ride back into the park at twenty below with feet like blocks of ice and hands that ached from the cold? "It takes a strange breed to live there," she said. "Some can, some can't."

Wintering in was easier for married people with good relationships who could tolerate several days of seeing no one but their spouses. Of course there were more isolated places to live in the United States, even in the modern era—Wyoming ranches, Alaska Native villages, and national park units in Utah. I would not choose a more isolated place than Lake, or one with no neighbors. It was too hard on a relationship to depend upon one's mate for everything. At Lake, we had other people to talk to. I had come to love my life at Lake, a challenging job as a ranger-naturalist in the summer, and skiing and lots of productive solitude in the winter. A Myers-Briggs personality profile I took as part of my naturalist training indicated I had become more introverted, and I could feel it. After so many months of solitude, my social skills seemed to atrophy and maybe my brain cells as well. Where was the creative edge I had discovered during my last big emotional upheaval? At Lake, I had vast overflowing quantities of serenity to share with troubled friends and relatives. However, recalling the muskrat our geology class saw floating on the ice floe in the Yellowstone River, I wondered if life was passing me by while I nibbled at the delicacies stuck there in the ice. What great falls awaited me ahead?

Of course, I didn't have to cope with a child, which would have accentuated the isolation. Taking a child outside in the winter presented formidable obstacles. While someone might be accustomed to carrying a heavy camera, water, and food on her back, putting a baby on his or her front made skiing challenging. Even going down to pick up the mail could be a problem for a mother home alone. I felt bewildered by the Carters' decision and, perhaps if I dared to admit it, a little smug. Looking around at our neighbors who had lived this life for so many years, I thought, "We could take it. We adapted." I didn't dare share those thoughts out loud, however. I didn't know the details of their decision; we certainly understood when another neighbor left after serious female health problems. Besides, I had learned that the universe punished me for gloating, invariably teaching me lessons in humility.

I was fairly sure that Terry still liked living in the park. He once casually mentioned that if I were ever ready to leave, I should let him know; he got bored with the long, ten-hour runs over Sylvan when the weather was not challenging enough. But then the park sent him and two of the rangers to gunnery school in Washington, where he learned to shoot an avalanche gun. When he returned, he enthusiastically demonstrated how to load a 75-millimeter recoilless rifle, invisible to me on the kitchen floor. He talked on and on, telling me everything he learned about safety. They had to store the three parts separately (the breech at Lake and the barrel and artillery shells up on the pass) so they could not be shanghaied by terrorists or used by criminals to blow up Pahaska Tepee. He learned that the ammunition was left over from the Korean War, so about a quarter of the rounds would be duds. If a dud did not leave the gun, it could explode. That would not be good.

Lois Lounsbury helped him make the long groomer runs feel shorter by sharing her collection of books on tape, including tales of Horatio Hornblower and the history of Genghis Khan (*The Devil's Horsemen*). And he really liked working for his new boss, Bruce Sefton, the Lake maintenance supervisor. With his hard work and his soft heart, Bruce was a good addition to the community. One year, he forgot to get anything for his wife, Melinda, for Valentine's Day so he snowmobiled to the East Entrance, drove fifty miles to Cody, bought a bouquet, put it in an icebox to keep it warm, and turned around for the eighty-mile return trip. And they had been married for close to twenty years! Melinda was also a great addition to the community. She was a devoted, tenderhearted friend of wildlife; at their previous home, she had talked a family of mice living in their attic into her hand, one by one, and carried them to safety. Somehow the animals knew her reputation: One day she and I were snowmobiling up to Sylvan Pass to watch Terry shoot the avalanche gun when suddenly a Clark's nutcracker flew across our path and dropped a mouse. I was sure the precious morsel was an offering of love to Melinda, friend of all the animals.

The Seftons had arrived at a bad time for wildlife lovers, however. The park estimated that in January and the first half of February 1989, the harsh winter had killed 262 elk, 15 bison, 1 moose, 4 pronghorn antelope, 2 sheep, 1 swan, and 2 coyotes. It was a good year for the predators. The park service no longer killed hundreds of elk and bison, as they had in the Chapmans' and Murphys' eras, so without either hunting or wolves to keep the population down, winter was their only predator. I knew we had too many animals. In the long run, winterkill benefited the ecosystem. I just wished the critters wouldn't die one by one before our eyes. When Melinda, Lorie, and I were out skiing on a bitterly cold day, a little herd of yearling bison followed us. We all felt bad, especially about the smallest one, still orange and the size of my golden retriever, obviously too young to survive the winter; his mother had drowned after falling through the ice. Terry teased Bruce that he would come home to find Melinda had moved them all into their garage.

We didn't have to live on canned goods as the Chapmans had, but Melinda learned the hard way about transporting food. After the thrill of getting airborne while snowmobiling over drifts, she screamed when she opened her icebox. The gallon of milk had split and two dozen eggs had broken, leaving the brown sugar, peanuts, and her best leather wallet floating in gooey eggnog. Parents had it worse, of course. When they went to town for the weekend, they also had to pack the crib, diapers, favorite teddy bear, and baby blankets.

One night the Seftons invited us to their house for a potluck. The biggest story was the snowmobiler who died after slamming into a bison in the dark. Apparently the snowmobile was going about eighty miles an hour; we figured he had been drinking. Next, we started the perennial recitation of mail delivery woes. Bruce and Melinda had just received a warning letter from the phone company saying their service was about to be cut off, and they would have to pay reconnection charges. They had mailed their check, via snowmobile courier, three weeks earlier. At that time, Yellowstone sometimes gave all the mail to volunteers from Mammoth to carry into the park. The couriers often carried thousands of dollars in paychecks and other payments, and we did not think the job should be given to volunteers. One time the volunteer couriers decided the weather was too stormy; they dropped off all the mail, including paychecks, at Norris. Alice said that one time her incoming mail, including checks, was left in a bag in the Mammoth fire cache for a week.

After trading a few such stories, Bruce muttered, "What are we doing here? There's only a handful of people crazy enough to live like this." Why did we do it? Were we just crazy as Bruce suggested? Were we just stuck, as Lorie suggested? At the Seftons' gathering, we shared a postcard from one of our summer neighbors, Carol Shively. The card showed thirteen lanes of traffic in Los Angeles, bumper to bumper. Carol liked to tell a story of the naturalist John Muir, who as a child fell into a dry well with poisonous gases. When his father found him and lowered a bucket, Muir's muddled brain had grown content in the well. "Get in the bucket! Get in the bucket!" his father exhorted him. Finally the logic registered, and he climbed into the bucket. Carol spent much of her childhood in Los Angeles and escaped to become a park ranger-naturalist. To her, the story explained how some city people could get trapped in intolerable living conditions. Their brains became so muddled by carbon monoxide that they couldn't recognize a bucket when they saw one. But could it also explain our staying at Lake?

Of all the people I interviewed in Yellowstone, no one admitted to suffering from cabin fever. I took a perverse interest in watching for its symptoms. Amongst our contemporaries at Lake, I only heard one man admit, one time, to feeling "stir crazy." We heard of one case where a couple divorced and lived separately for several years. When he left the park, they remarried. Reading an article in the Northern Lights literary magazine one day, I found a phrase to remember. It defined cabin fever as "an intense state of irrational immobility."

Maybe cabin fever wasn't boredom after all. After enjoying the ladies' lunches so much the first three winters, it seemed quite irrational that we had not continued the tradition. Why had it become so difficult some days for me to summon the energy to return phone calls? I thought one guy was trying to prove how tough he was, spending the winter alone and refusing our invitations to potlucks, but maybe he just couldn't summon the energy. Why had we started going out of the park less frequently? At first we substituted ski trips to backcountry cabins or tours of Old Faithful, but often we just stayed home. Did "irrational immobility" explain why we stayed so many years in Yellowstone?

Despite the forced togetherness and lack of privacy in the small community, any self-doubts were generally hidden behind a facade of bravado, which I felt was designed to fool ourselves as much as anyone else. We used the conventional definition of cabin fever: boredom in its milder forms and complete mental breakdowns at its most severe. We took pride in measuring our own tolerance against stories of suicides and murders in Yellowstone long ago, when the seclusion was absolute and knew no solace.

Our gatherings at Lake gave us the opportunity to trade stories and vent our frustrations through humor, and I looked forward to having the Reinharts there to contribute their own stories. Not all the Yellowstone interior communities had such gatherings, especially where the women lived outside the park. The men's lives in those communities were oriented towards weekend reunions with their families, not towards building community. With just twelve people living at Lake, our secrets were few. We sought each other's counsel for flu remedies, sick housecats, coughing snowmobiles, and broken hearts. Those who cared to look through the clear garbage bags stacked in the maintenance shop knew who had been eating lots of Swanson TV dinners. On mail days, we saw who received Victoria's Secrets catalogs, the Sierra Club magazine, or National Enquirer. We knew who had been trying to have a baby and why they couldn't, who had to be strapped onto his snowmobile to make it home after a drinking binge, and whose dog was peeing on whose snowmobiles.

At the same time, we tried to recognize the fine line between offering a shoulder to cry on and taking sides in disputes. Our knowledge of each other's lives could have been ammunition if we had warring factions. Fortunately at Lake, we all got along, and there was very little turnover. A community spirit is fragile, however: If one employee left, and his or her replacement was bad tempered, it threatened turmoil for all of us. We watched other communities function like a bunch of poisonous snakes. A mistake blown out of proportion left someone in tears and looking for revenge.

I was optimistic about Karen and Dan as new members of our community and eager to help them. Fortunately, they did not have to come over Sylvan on that frigid January day. After eight and a half years and four snowmobiles, I finally had a dependable machine, a Ski-doo 440 long track. I dressed carefully for the trip and laughed at how foolish I had been years earlier when I dressed like the Michelin man and wore a heavy daypack on my back instead of strapped to the machine. Lorie would be proud of me if she could see me now, venturing out by myself pulling a sled. I dressed in polypropylene long underwear to wick moisture away from my body. On my feet I wore Sorel Pacs with thick felt liners (and shocking pink shoelaces to distinguish mine from everyone else's at group gatherings). Inside my sheepskin mittens, I had learned to wear polypropylene gloves. On this really cold day, I wore a neoprene facemask and a polypro balaclava. I grew up when "plastic" was a dirty word: If I read those chemicals on a bread wrapper, I would throw it back on the shelf in revulsion. But as the man told a skeptical Dustin Hoffman in the movie *The Graduate*, plastics represented the future. A reluctant convert, I had to admit that "plastics" made snowmobilers warmer and firefighters safer in their Nomex clothing.

When I arrived at the Mammoth parking lot, the temperature was about 10°, without wind chill. I couldn't start our truck, so I ate my frozen peanut butter and jelly sandwich in the cold cab, out of the wind, wondering whether we should even attempt taking the baby and the dog in to Lake. I met the Reinharts and we managed to pack their gear onto the two sleds: all the infant necessities plus three weeks' worth of groceries and laundered clothes. The fates did not seem to be smiling upon us, however. The track on their Yamaha was frozen, and it took us half an hour of dragging the machine around and shoving it over on its side to free it. Dan's government machine got stuck. When both sleds were packed, Emma was packed into her Snugli and then into her mother's oversized snowmobile suit. Everyone else was ready to go, but my throttle-cable linkage separated, which took several minutes to fix with ungloved, stiff fingers.

All of us felt apprehensive. With temperatures that low, there was little margin for error. Like me, Karen had always disdained the noisy contraption, which she referred to as a "crotch rocket." I knew from experience that snowmobiling required at least a few miles to learn. Karen would be transporting either the baby or the dog, Ebony, whose riding ability was also untested. I imagined Ebony being as difficult as our dog, Tucker, who habitually squirmed and leaned against Terry's arms the entire trip. At least Ebony didn't have Tucker's giant bat-like ears, which often blocked Terry's vision. Dan and Karen knew that other babies had ridden inside snowmachine suits, but they didn't quite believe their precious Emma could breathe under all those layers. I imagined one of the machines breaking down and then trying to flag someone down to get the baby to safety. With the winds I had encountered at Swan Lake flats, I thought Hayden Valley roads might have drifted over. Once we got going, however, the hour-and-a-half trip went smoothly. Ebon laid down for the trip, nearly snoozing even when we rode through a bison herd. At the first stop, Karen said exuberantly, "I think I was a snowmobiler in a past life!" Her only complaint was how hot her hands felt. Although we encountered several pairs of bison and finally a herd of cows and calves, none became feisty.

We arrived at Lake just in time to unload the sleds before dark. After being outside for eight hours, I felt tired and hungry but elated. We delivered the baby and the dog without incident! Thinking about how much I had changed over the past eight and a half years, I looked forward to watching Emma grow up in the park and seeing how Yellowstone shaped her. After unloading the sled, I followed Terry's rule and gassed and oiled my machine. He said it should be ready in case of emergency. I used to call him Mr. Overprepared, but his planning had saved our necks more than once over our winters in the park, so I went through the motions anyway.

I looked forward to sitting beside the fire with a glass of wine, but it was not to be. When I arrived at the apartment building, Dan delivered a message from Terry, who had just called on the radio. He was having snowmachine trouble and wanted me to meet him on Sylvan Pass. Imagining him stranded there in the cold, I hurriedly packed a flashlight, a couple of bungee cords, and some sheepskin-lined mitts for his frozen hands. As I rode out in the dark, I fumbled to find the high-beam switch on the headlights. We rarely traveled after dark, especially when it was that cold. As I careened toward Fishing Bridge at fifty-five miles per hour, I glimpsed a movement on the bridge. Maybe I had time to find the headlight switch after all. We didn't want a rescue expedition for me and him. Indeed, a little herd of bison cows and calves were on the bridge. I passed them and a confused calf started galloping ahead of me. I briefly wondered whether it was wise to ride between the mom and the baby, but I had to concentrate on the six animals ahead of me rather than the one mom behind me in the dark.

At Mary Bay, I caught sight of a lone figure waving his arm in the red glow of his taillight. No headlight at all. How in the world had Terry made it all the way without lights? Later he told me he used a flashlight to warn a group of approaching snowmachines. "Are you going to be all right?" one asked him incredulously. He amused himself thinking he should have said, "Sure, I'm a maintenance worker. I've been driving like this all winter." Although the sky was overcast, the moon lit the road much better than the night I had walked off the pass. Terry figured he was fine unless he ran into an albino moose at Cub Creek. At Mary Bay, his flashlight burned out so he called for help.

"Aren't you tired of snowmobiling yet?" he shouted over the roar of the machines and the wind. I just grinned, thinking I was glad to be the rescuer instead of the rescuee for once. We headed home, me on the left side of the road and his machine on the right, glad for the day's adventures to be over.

CHAPTER EIGHTEEN
A Bend in the Road

It's not so much that we're afraid of change or so in love with the old ways, but it's that place in between that we fear....It's like being between trapezes.

—MARILYN FERGUSON, AMERICAN FUTURIST

*F*AMILIAR SCENES DRIFTED BEFORE ME, THE TEMPO shifting with Will Ackerman's guitar on the cassette tape: a coyote trotting along a snowy lakeshore. An elk alone on a bluff, its muzzle sniffing the snow-filled wind. The tranquil images, combined with the Novocain, lulled me almost to sleep in the dentist's chair, despite the grinding and chipping. Yet when he asked me to rank the stress in my life on a scale from one to ten, I sheepishly answered, "Five."

After nine years, we had learned that all our Lake neighbors got kind of grumpy in the fall. The park would stop plowing and sanding roads weeks before we could begin snowmobiling, and we had to get our winter supplies into the park before that happened. Summer 1993 had been short; it snowed every week through the Fourth of July, and Terry actually plowed snow off Sylvan Pass that day.

At work at the Fishing Bridge Visitor Center, I spotted a job announcement for the heavy equipment operator/supervisor at Mesa Verde National Park. As I stared at it I realized this was the only job at the only other park that Terry would consider. Nearly every spring during our years in Yellowstone, Terry and I had escaped to the southwestern United States, and we had talked vaguely about moving there someday—someplace with an elevation low enough that we could have fruit trees. We enjoyed the cultural diversity where you could hear Spanish, Navajo, and Ute in the grocery store. One year we stopped by Mesa Verde National Park and talked with the maintenance foreman, but the heavy equipment operators there liked their jobs, and there wasn't much turnover.

I realized I had to take the job announcement home to Terry. After nine years in Yellowstone, I felt I could stay for the rest of my life. But as I watched Terry read the announcement, I could see he was ready for a new challenge. Years ago, he often said, "Can you believe I get paid to do this?" but he had not said that for a while now. Books on tape no longer kept him from being bored on the long grooming runs. He had been ready for some time; I had ignored the clues. Trying to hold back my tears and share his enthusiasm, I suddenly had to walk the dog. Once outside, the tears flowed as I began my grieving, alone. My stomach reeled. I never read job announcements. Why did I notice this one? Why did I take it home?

I loved Lake, the lifestyle, and the community. But I had chosen Terry because he was building an airplane in his basement. He had a sense of adventure and a love for travel, which I had always shared. In the past, I had never worked anywhere longer than seven years; I didn't want to be the stolid one who resisted change. I could hardly expect him to stay for seven more years, until retirement, just for me; it wouldn't necessarily even be best for me. My history and my heritage demanded that I, too, seek new frontiers.

Unlike in other places, no one can stay in Yellowstone National Park forever. The only question was when and how you left.

That night I dreamed of jumping off a cliff with someone. I felt terribly frightened but exhilarated. The next day, I told Karen Reinhart about the Mesa Verde job opening. Karen and I had become fast friends that year, skiing or walking together each evening with little Emma in her Snugli. Obviously upset, she muttered that I shouldn't have told her so soon; Terry hadn't gotten the job yet. We both knew such positions were very competitive, and most applications were filed for naught. While I took hope for a moment, I knew in my gut that she was wrong. With his skills, his ability to manage a crew, and his unblemished safety record, Terry would get the job. When the Mesa Verde foreman called Terry's boss, Bruce Sefton, for a reference, normally pleasant Bruce snapped, "Yeah, what do you want? I know you're going to take him, and you're going to kill me." Bruce had been a dream boss and a good friend, and Terry knew he wasn't likely to find such a good supervisor again.

When Mesa Verde offered Terry the position, he was jubilant. He had reason to be. He wanted a change, and the offer affirmed his abilities. "Remember," he said, "everyone says there are only two good parks. The one you just left, and the one you are going to." The following three weeks were a blur of activity with little time for grieving as we bought a house in Mancos, Colorado, prepared for the moving van, and said our goodbyes. In a trance, I took my camera through the Fishing Bridge Visitor Center's bird exhibits where I had watched parents introduce their children to the natural world so many times. Walking alone down the beach of the most beautiful lake in North America, I heard trumpeter swans and saw seventeen of them, returning for the winter.

I was leaving, and there were so many things I hadn't done yet—visited the Thorofare ranger station where Dave and Kathleen lived, made a good audio tape of the lake freezing, successfully photographed swans in flight, climbed Avalanche Peak. There had always been tomorrow. Then I remembered Ranger Jerry Mernin who, after more than twenty years in the park, had not completed his Yellowstone list; he still wanted to ride the Continental Divide through the park.

On the way back from our last trip to Bozeman, Montana, to buy groceries, we watched a bull elk nudge fifteen dawdling cows and calves across the road. Moonlight shining through the steam of fumaroles nearly overwhelmed me with a flood of nostalgia and regret. Then we passed the corner where my snowmachine broke down the last time. Terry figured we had put $10,000 into buying snowmachines over the years, each time throwing the money into a black hole. We had 5,100 miles on the Polaris and 3,500 miles on the Ski Doo, and we had never taken them outside the park. I remembered Yellowstone Lake in a storm, the ugliest, scariest lake in the world. A favorite Bozeman treat—almond-filled croissants—tasted stale for the first time.

On the poster announcing our farewell party, Karen drew our van with three heads inside—Terry's, mine, and our bat-eared dog Tucker's—rolling down the road toward cliff dwellings and leaving skis behind. Seeing it, my eyes filled again. I had convinced myself that three of us would be going but three of us would be staying—clones perhaps? The poster image brought home the truth. The past nine years had been the happiest in my life. At the farewell party at the Lounsburys' house, my clone smiled and laughed cheerfully with friends and acquaintances, grown dear after years of shared triumphs and sacrifices. I watched her, bewildered.

In accordance with the Yellowstone tradition for farewell parties, our neighbors and friends took turns telling stories. Their gentle teasing created a verbal vignette of our community's life in the heart of Yellowstone. Lester and Inez Warwood sent a card saying they would always be grateful to Terry for his quick thinking—and his sharp knife —when the barge almost pulled Lester's boat to the depths of the lake. Ranger Bob Mahn talked about how much he suffered watching Terry, the park's lightest heavy equipment operator, eat a huge lunch without consequences to his waistline. Many of the faces from our earliest years in the park weren't there: Bob and Alice Roller had retired; Chris and Hume Lilley took a hardship transfer to another park because of her asthma; Lorie Rippley married a rancher and started a family in Montana. Only a few of our friends seemed likely to stay until retirement—John and Lois Lounsbury, Jerry and Cindy Mernin, and Bob Mahn and his wife, Grace Nutting. Lois was unusually quiet. Cindy just said, "Bah, humbug." They both had attended far too many farewell parties. As we left, Bruce joked, "By the way, did you hear the news? Mesa Verde burned up. It's all gone. You'll have to stay." We tried to laugh.

On November 18 a voracious winter storm nearly swallowed our moving van, chasing us out of the park. The snow fell thickly off and on and wind blew enough to make the hairs on the back of Terry's neck stand, once again. The weather was a blessing since it forced me to keep my eyes focused forward instead of backward. The park had stopped plowing the roads for the season, so we had to leave now or never. There was already a foot of new snow on the road. Terry made tracks with our four-wheel drive pickup truck, pulling the trailer, and I followed in the minivan, the van's front bumper plowing snow off the road and into the windshield. I kept brushing the tears out of my eyes as I strained to see. How could we be leaving this place?

As I pulled onto Bridge Bay flats a few miles down the road, however, the sun burst through, and fickle Yellowstone put on her kind face. I put in a cassette tape of Phil Heywood singing "Summertime," the same tape we had played for our wedding. As I pulled up the hill, Phil crooned, "One of these mornings, you're going to wake up singing, you're going to spread your wings, and you're going to fly. Until that morning, ain't nothin' can harm you, so hush little baby, don't you cry." Phil's familiar voice gradually dried my tears and delivered a sudden, unexpected sensation—liberation? No more fighting off winter to get the last load of groceries home. No more bananas squashed to a pulp on the snowmachine sled. No more asphyxiating snowmobile rides. Now we could plan social outings without the subjective trailer on our sentences... "if the weather holds."

As we settled into Mancos, we celebrated every day we were able to walk to the post office and the library instead of snowmobiling fifty miles. Terry liked working at Mesa Verde with its new challenges and the nice heavy machinery, compared with the old equipment at Lake. I finally had access to email and realized what a difference email and internet would have made to all of us in the park interior. I also could reconnect with my sister and her family in the South Pacific.

Mancos Valley acquaintances who had visited Yellowstone and dreamed about living there could not understand why we left. Living at Lake, behind the gates, the people in our community had a different relationship with the park, we explained. We had to snowmobile fifty miles before we could buy a carton of milk, eat a restaurant meal, or visit a friend, regardless of conditions. We said the winters did not bother us nearly as much as the interminable springs. We really did not discuss our deeper feelings. In Yellowstone, we lived on the edge, coming to terms with the danger and the isolation in our own ways. But for our trip back in time, we weren't restricted to a one-way ticket. We had a choice to return to civilization, and for various reasons, we did.

Nine years on the winter's frontier had transformed me and everyone I knew there. I could barely recognize the woman who had whined and bitched so much about that first trip over Sylvan in 1984. I learned Terry was the perfect companion for that place where we were forced to spend so much time in one another's company, often under stressful conditions. I learned the long stretches of uninterrupted time posed as much of a challenge as the occasional moments of sheer terror. I had come to appreciate snowmobiles—the blasted contraptions—because we were not nearly as isolated as the Chapmans, Murphys, and Mernins.

In a city, we often can choose to spend time with people in the same age group who share our politics, environmental values, and tastes. Our Lake community consisted of a hodgepodge of different values and lifestyles. But because we shared a unique way of life, we tried to appreciate each person's unique qualities. After living in the park, I wasn't quite so quick to be self-righteous about people's choices. We found out frontier life demanded not strong-willed independence but interdependence. We banded together against the common enemy, whether it was headquarters, the thief who stole Lorie's snowmobile sled, the fires, or the damned snowmobiles.

We all at various times found the long Yellowstone winter an incompatible bedfellow. After we left the park, we heard more about emotional scars and realized we had not known everything about each other after all. After successfully putting up the front for several winters, one of our friends eventually sought treatment for a compulsive eating disorder. We knew that several people over the years drank too much, but we did not know the rangers had found one of our neighbors floating in his boat, totally blacked out. Although we recognized that such problems can occur anywhere, we wondered how much the extreme isolation contributed to them. Others suffered physical scars. I thought of Alice Roller who suffered every day from her snowmobile accidents, and of the thousands of dollars spent by employees on chiropractors and joint replacements caused by too many miles squatting on snowmobiles.

Those who successfully adjusted to Yellowstone gave up, to

some degree, the illusion of controlling their lives. A few of our neighbors stubbornly resisted this lesson, refusing to wear long underwear even under extreme conditions and continuing with their plans, regardless of the cold. They ended up with frostbitten cheeks, dark patches as big as silver dollars, or worse. We became "flexitarian," admitting that Mother Nature was boss. Yellowstone provided the serenity to accept the things we could not change about our surroundings and about each other.

Yellowstone was a difficult, demanding teacher; but her lessons and the friends we made in her classroom would last a lifetime. We treasured our Yellowstone friends' phone calls and visits. In Mancos, I never tied up a trash bag without imagining Lorie racing her cohorts in the Trash Can Boogie. Every time we pulled out our Bob-Mahn–sized plastic dinner plates for a potluck dinner, we thought about Bob and his huge appetite for life. I never closed the toilet seat in the night without thinking of the Mernins. When the Reinharts came to Colorado, we enjoyed seeing their little wilderness baby Emma. While other children learning to talk can bark like a dog or moo like a cow, this offspring of Yellowstone had learned to howl like a coyote, grunt like a bison, and growl like a grizzly.

After less than two months in Mancos, I started to question my perception of danger. No one anywhere knows how many times they escape death by a nanosecond: a car careening into your lane, a collision with a snowboard on the slope, a lightning strike from a cloudless sky on your mountaintop. After we left, there was a fatal accident in the Northwest involving an old Army 75-millimeter recoilless, an avalanche gun using shells manufactured during the Korean War, just like the ones Terry and the crew used on Sylvan. A shell exploded and blew the gun apart, killing a person on the platform. After that Yellowstone got a howitzer, a newer and safer alternative for avalanche control.

But that was just the avalanche gun. Terry had not been elec-

trocuted by the generator, eaten by a bear, or buried in an avalanche. Had I exaggerated the risks to Terry and others? In the
outside world, help was just around the corner. Even Mancos—a
town of 1,000 people—had its own volunteer fire department,
ambulance service, medical clinic, and dentist. As I read adventure books from the library, I found it hard to believe the vulner-
ability and interdependence we felt there. Maybe we had been de-
luding ourselves. Despite all the A&W Adventures, neither Terry
nor I had even been injured there.

Then on January 17, 1994, we received the call from Cindy
Mernin. "There was an accident this morning. Bob Mahn was
snowmobiling up to check Sylvan and went off the road. He's
dead."

CHAPTER NINETEEN

Grinning Amongst the Titans

I can't be contented with yesterday's glory,
I can't live on promises winter to spring;
Today is my moment and now is my story,
I'll laugh and I'll cry and I'll sing.

FROM SONG "TODAY" BY PAUL KANTNER

OTHING SEEMS AS INNOCENT AS A SINGLE FLAKE OF snow. Falling slowly, silently, it covers blemishes and masks sounds on the landscape, delivering tranquility. Pressing my nose against the glass as a child, I remember my delight at the first snow each fall. Growing up in a family of skiers, I shared anticipation for the first snowfall, as eagerly as for Christmas. I was sixteen before I lost my innocence. Feeling a car fishtail with me at the wheel for the first time, I realized snow's malevolence. Not long after that my family was caught in a snow slide. I was horrified at the heavy, wet cement that tried to smother my sister Becky.

In Yellowstone, skiing and snowmobiling depended upon adequate snow. Yet sometimes it fell too hard, too quickly, avalanching from the sky. Employees who lived year-round in the park came to understand Yellowstone's life or death power over their lives. With them tempting the fates every day at hazardous locations, occasionally the odds caught up with park employees. Yet death always came as a horrifying revelation. Bob Mahn was no stranger to death. As a ranger and a volunteer Emergency Medical Technician (EMT), he had faced it over the bodies of accident victims many times, often victoriously. His wife, Grace Nutting, and the two other rangers at the East Gate, learned much of what they knew about emergencies from working alongside Bob, an EMT instructor.

As the East Gate ranger, Bob Mahn had been checking Sylvan Pass every morning for twelve years and was intimately familiar with "The Lady's" curves and treacheries. Now the guardian of Sylvan Pass was dead, a victim of the pass he knew better than anyone. How could it be? Bob, the first Yellowstone National Park person I met upon my arrival in the park. Bob, who taught Terry about Sylvan Pass over dozens of lunches at Pahaska Tepee. Bob Mahn, a mountain of a man. How could that power have dissolved into nothing overnight? Bob, the fifty-one-year-old husband of Grace. Grace...how would she possibly survive?

Hanging up the phone after Cindy's call, Terry and I crumpled into each other's arms. We felt so alienated, so far from our friends in Yellowstone. After dozens of phone calls over the following days, we pieced together the story of his death. When Bob set out on his snowmobile at 7:15 A.M., Grace said, "Goodbye, dear. Be careful," and then she fell back asleep. At 8 A.M., the phone jangled her awake, and she knew immediately something awful had happened. It was the Lake groomer, Phil Anderson, saying he couldn't reach Bob on the radio. With all the dead spots for radio signals on the pass, that wouldn't have been surprising. But the communication center at Mammoth couldn't even get background noise from his radio. Grace mumbled that he must have dropped his radio in the snow, but deep in her stomach, she knew she was kidding herself. With the first rush of adrenaline, she called Bob Coe at Pahaska Tepee and asked him to get some sleds ready—"just in case." Hearing the radio traffic, the other East Gate ranger, Arthur Jawad, broke in and said he was going up.

Although Bob had left less than an hour earlier, Arthur could barely make out his tracks in the blowing snow. Fifteen inches had fallen overnight, and four inches lay on top of Bob's tracks. Sylvan was as bad as Arthur had ever seen it—twenty-mile-an-hour winds whipping the snow. In his mind Arthur had planned such a mission on Sylvan dozens of times, especially after getting caught in an avalanche himself the year before. He half expected one of the rangers to go off the steep-sided pass. But Bob's tracks didn't go over the cliff; they dove into a gulley on an inside curve. Reporting on his radio, Arthur knew that Grace was the only one at the station to relay calls, and she was the last person he wanted to talk to at that moment. "I'm five miles up the road," he said in a forced, steady voice. "Do you want to hear the particulars?" "Yes," she said. "I can see where he went off the edge, and there's a (snowmachine) ski sticking out. I'm going down."

After relaying the information to the communication center at Mammoth, Grace and Julia Jawad frantically gathered marker flags and shovels and jumped onto a snowmachine. As they careened up the road, Grace prayed for strength. Bob Coe followed with two of his employees from Pahaska, and somehow, despite the conditions, Ranger John Lounsbury made it over the pass from Lake. Grace lunged into the pit along with the men as they pushed and dragged their 250-pound friend up the cliff and onto the sled for the trip to the plowed road. As the snowmachine pulled the sled, Grace and Arthur alternated doing CPR, desperately shoving Bob's massive chest against his heart and pouring their breath into his lungs. Long after it was clear that Bob was gone, his wife and his partner continued their efforts, not wanting to believe that their years of training and their passionate attempts would fail on this, the man they most wanted to save. The autopsy indicated that a blow to his head had knocked him out, and then he had suffocated from the snow. His snowmobile helmet was deeply dented from hitting either a tree or the snowmachine.

That night I awakened angry and frightened by the suddenness with which Grace had lost her husband. Any of us could be in her shoes overnight. While her pain and anger simmered visibly, her courage was also clear. I attributed her strength to the fact that before Bob, she spent many years alone; and thus she knew she could. She also had many other passions—writing, reading, birding. I felt immensely thankful we had left Yellowstone. Terry reacted differently, of course. Bob's death made him renew his pledge to live each day fully. "Most of our friends make it, but some of them don't," he said, his eyes shining with tears.

I remembered Bob rosy cheeked and grinning on Sylvan after a storm, tossing our heavy, old snowmachine back into the track like it was a toy. Bob had seemed most at home there in the Absarokas, and I could picture him there still, grinning among the titans. Grace called after the service at Lake on January 20. She had snowmobiled over Sylvan to attend the service, forcing herself to stop at the pit where Bob had died and show it to her sisters. She felt gratified with the turnout, hundreds of snowmobiles congregating at the Lake Ranger Station, including the park superintendent and the chief ranger. Although Jerry Mernin had attended too many funerals for colleagues in his years with the Park Service, his voice broke as he talked about Bob. He offered the old French slogan, "mort cheval au galop." Bob had died "on horseback," doing the work he loved.

Even more people attended Bob's cemetery service outside the park near Cody. At the graveside, Grace tenderly placed two of Bob's old railroad lanterns in the grave. Remembering Bob's love for food and firefighting, Phil Anderson contributed an

MRE. An eagle circled the funeral procession and seemed to follow it, soaring with the mountain currents. We were sure it was Bob. For months afterward, Grace's chest muscles continued to ache; she said it was from the exertion of trying CPR. I figured it was her broken heart. We watched the video of the memorial service alone in Mancos. The twenty-one-gun salute shattered the serenity of the frozen, silent lake. A lone trumpet played taps as they lowered the flag and handed it to Grace. At least she would have something to hold. As the silence amplified the pain in the Lake Ranger Station, we heard a familiar sound—Emma Reinhart, growling like a grizzly.

Epilogue

For the first couple of years that Grace Nutting came to visit us in Mancos, Bob Mahn came, too. Our conversations centered on him in old, familiar stories. Terry said he and Bob had joked about Sylvan taking one of them someday, but then Terry shoved the thought to a dark corner and forgot it. Grace realized Bob's job was dangerous but didn't dwell upon it; she figured Bob could handle anything that came up. After his death, she realized that was false confidence. Yellowstone's teeth bit home.

Yellowstone National Park and its management policies continued evolving after we left, just as they had from the park's beginning. The biggest change was the reintroduction of wolves. While once Ranger Scotty Chapman and other rangers killed coyotes and elk as part of their assigned duties, later park managers focused on trying to establish a more naturally functioning ecosystem. Bears had to make an honest living out in the woods rather than being fed garbage by people like Henry Rahn. In 1995, two years after we left the park, Yellowstone introduced fourteen gray wolves from Alberta, Canada. When we visited Yellowstone, we joined the hordes of other tourists striving to catch a glimpse of wolves or to hear their eerie howls. More importantly, biologists said Yellowstone's biodiversity dramatically improved. At the end of 2011, there were at least ninety-eight wolves in Yellowstone.

In 2011, a total of 3.4 million people visited Yellowstone, including 88,804 in the winter—up to 720 snowmobiles per day. Who could have anticipated that overuse in the winter would become a problem when the Mernins lived at Lake in the 1970s, much less when the Chapmans and the Murphys lived there in the 1930s and 1950s? Four years after we left the park in 1997, the Fund for Animals filed a lawsuit to ban all snow grooming of paved roads in the park. Subsequently, the park severely limited snowmobiling, partially to reduce air and noise pollution and partially to protect wildlife. This immersed park managers in controversy once again as border communities and visitors wanted the open access they had enjoyed in the past. The debate focused in part on the dangerous Sylvan Pass as well as on snowmobiles' noise and emissions. Some mentioned Ranger Bob Mahn's death in their arguments for more restrictions. This would have infuriated Bob, who advocated more access for the hardy, local people with limited resources, some of whom had snowmobiled into the park before the roads were ever groomed. The park initially proposed allowing no snowmobiling, but the state of Wyoming and the border towns' chambers of commerce opposed that change. At this writing, most winter visitors had to be guided through the park, but the winter use policy was still evolving.

Our giant former neighbor, Yellowstone Lake, changed more in the twenty years since we had left than it had for thousands of previous years. Someone (probably a fisherman) evidently introduced a non-native fish, lake trout, which decimated the population of the iconic, genetically pure, Yellowstone cutthroat trout. Anglers could no longer count on catching cutthroat in the numbers we had enjoyed. More important were the impacts on forty-two species that depend upon cutthroat, including grizzlies, eagles, osprey, pelicans, and otters. The lake trout live in deep water, making them unavailable to most anglers and animals. When we visited in 2012, there were no osprey nests in the Lake area for the first time in decades. Each summer, park contractors kill hundreds of thousands of lake trout there in an attempt to save the cutthroat, but at this writing, it still was not clear whether they will succeed.

The fires of 1988 caused many changes to Yellowstone, but neither the park nor the tourist traffic was devastated, as had been feared. In fact, many visitors came to see for themselves what had happened. Visitors still can see the gray trunks of trees burned in 1988, but new forests tower over the visitors' heads. The forests regenerated naturally, with the lodgepole pine cones opening in the heat and spreading millions of seeds. Because fire continues to be part of the evolving park, it can be confusing. For example, a fire in 2008 near Sylvan Pass burned so hot that much of the seed bank was lost. That area might not recover for many years. In 1992, the park adopted a new fire policy, which still allows natural fires to burn unless they threaten human life or development. However, park managers now have to consider the regional and national fire situation, including the availability of firefighters and equipment. Yellowstone also increased its fire management staff so they would be better able to evaluate computer models and real-time weather data, according to Karen Wildung Reinhart in her book, *Yellowstone's Rebirth by Fire: Rising from the Ashes of the 1988 Wildfires*.

As the years went by, our friends established new lives, mostly outside the park, but often pondering their lives in Yellowstone and how that experience transformed them. Grace eventually settled into being single, traveling internationally on birding trips and working as a water master for the local irrigation district. In 1994, the first annual Bob Mahn Award was presented to East Entrance Ranger Arthur Jawad, who was honored for his dedication to public service.

Karen and Dan Reinhart spent five winters living at Lake with their children Emma and Forrest (born three years after Emma). She worked as a ranger-naturalist in Yellowstone and wrote two books on the park (the fire book and *Old Faithful Inn: Crown Jewel of National Park Lodges*). She now works for the Yellowstone Gateway Museum. She has three children. Lorie Rippley married, had two girls, and reinvented herself as an office worker, something she never expected to do. She says she quit talking about her adventures in Yellowstone because she felt no one believed her.

Terry worked at Mesa Verde National Park for one and a half years before taking early retirement in 1995. Bruce and Melinda Sefton still live and work at Lake. Many of us (Cindy Mernin, Alice Siebecker, and Lois Lounsbury) became enthusiastic gardeners after we left the park, trying to make up for all those years when we could not have gardens because they would attract bears or be trampled by bison. Cindy also found great joy in raising chickens.

Alice Siebecker married, had two boys, and retired from paid employment in 2007. She continues to operate informally as the Lake community social worker by organizing retirement and honoring parties. After surviving fires, poachers, and grizzly bears in Yellowstone for several decades, Dave Phillips and Kathleen O'Leary retired in 2006, and he died three years later of apparent heart failure at the age of sixty-three.

Like many of the people we knew, Jerry Mernin turned down many promotions in order to stay in Yellowstone, ultimately spending almost his entire forty-four-year National Park Service career there, ten years more than even Scotty Chapman. At the encouragement of numerous people, Jerry devoted his retirement to writing his memoir for the benefit of new generations of rangers. The book was headed for publication in 2013.

On December 13, 2011, five days before his fortieth anniversary with Cindy, Jerry died at the age of seventy-nine. Although he suffered from Parkinson's disease for several years, his mind, wit, and memory were unaffected to the end. We miss him. Hardly a week passes when we don't think of a story we shared with Jerry or a philosophical topic we long to discuss with him.

Terry and I attended the memorial parties for both Dave Phillips and Jerry Mernin at Lake. Former employees traveled from as far away as Alaska and the East Coast to remember them, trade stories, and be reunited with the Yellowstone family. Yellowstone's military roots shaped the Mernin memorial. A riderless horse with boots backward in the stirrups and a packhorse were led before the hushed crowd, followed by a twenty-one-gun salute.

As we discussed our experiences with friends and acquaintances at the memorials and reunions, we felt wistful, just as Scotty Chapman, Horace Albright, Alice Murphy, and others felt when we interviewed them after their retirements. Sure, we all recognized that Yellowstone is not for sissies. It has teeth, and many of us narrowly averted the bite. But after a few decades, the shadows faded, and sunshine tinted our memories. Our years in Yellowstone were indeed the good old days.

Bibliography

Bateson, Gerald L., Jr. *Growing up in Yellowstone*. Gardiner, Montana: Pumice Point Press, 2011.

Gonzales, Laurence. *Deep Survival: Who Lives, Who Dies, and Why*. W.W. Norton & Company, 2003.

Henry, Jeff. *Snowshoes, Coaches, and Cross Country Skis: A Brief History of Yellowstone Winters*. Emigrant, Montana: Roche Jaune Pictures, Inc., 2011.

Kaufman, Polly Welts. *National Parks and the Woman's Voice: A History*. Albuquerque: University of New Mexico Press, updated in 2006.

Reinhart, Karen Wildung. *Yellowstone's Rebirth by Fire: Rising from the Ashes of the 1988 Wildfires*. Helena, Montana: Farcountry Press, 2008.

Reinhart, Karen Wildung and Henry, Jeff. *Old Faithful Inn: Crown Jewel of National Park Lodges*. Emigrant, Montana: Roche Jaune Pictures, Inc. 2004.

Riley, Glenda. *The Female Frontier: A Comparative View of Women on the Prairie and the Plains*. Lawrence: University Press of Kansas, 1988.

Schlissel, Lillian. *Women's Diaries of the Westward Journey*. New York: Schocken Books, 1982.

Schullery, Paul. *The Bears of Yellowstone*. Boulder, Colorado: Roberts Rinehart, 1986.

Watry, Elizabeth. *Women in Wonderland: Lives, Legends, and Legacies of Yellowstone National Park*. Helena, Montana: Riverbend Publishing, 2012.

Whittlesey, Lee H. *Death in Yellowstone: Accidents and Foolhardiness in the First National Park*. Boulder, Colorado: Roberts Rinehart, 1995.

About the Author

Marjane Ambler has been a journalist since 1968. She was an associate editor for *High Country News* (an environmental newspaper) from 1974-1980. In 1990 the University Press of Kansas published her first book, *Breaking the Iron Bonds: Indian Control of Energy Development.* From 1995 until 2006, she served as the editor of *Tribal College Journal* (a national quarterly magazine).

Marjane Ambler and her husband, Terry Wehrman, with their dog, Tucker. (1992 photo by Joan Earl)

Marjane and her husband, Terry Wehrman, lived in Yellowstone National Park year round from 1984 through 1993 and interviewed the other people included in *Yellowstone Has Teeth.* For four summers (1990-1993), Marjane served as a seasonal interpretative ranger for the National Park Service.

Now retired from the park service, Marjane and Terry divide the year between Atlantic City, Wyoming, not far from Yellowstone, and Lake Havasu, Arizona. Marjane's website is www.marjaneambler.com